Hang on
to Your
Hormones

Hang on
to Your
Hormones:
Straight Talk on
Sex, Love & Dating

Beverly J. Hadland

LIFE CYCLE BOOKS LTD.
Toronto, Ontario • Lewiston, New York

Hang on to Your Hormones: Straight Talk on Sex, Love & Dating.

Published by:
Life Cycle Books Ltd.
2205 Danforth Avenue
Toronto, Ontario
M4C 1K4
(416) 690-5860

U.S.A. Office
Life Cycle Books
P.O. Box 420
Lewiston, NY 14092-0420

Printed in Canada

Typesetting by All About Type, Toronto.

ISBN 0-919225-38-1

To Karen Roth-Tang, who as a student challenged her boss (me) physically, emotionally and spiritually because of her decision to wait until marriage before being sexually active. My life was never the same again. I thank God daily for Karen and for young people like her who have the guts to be different and stand up against what is wrong, no matter the cost!

Acknowledgments

Much of this book is written from my own experiences as well as from questions and solutions given to me from teenagers themselves. I am so excited to see that today's youth are much smarter about sex than we were years ago. Not only smarter but they are not buying into the Hollywood image. Our youth are sensitive and compassionate. More teens volunteer their time than adults. Many have gone through so much in their short years that some of us older ones could never handle. So here's to the youth of the 90s!

I'd also like to thank Evelyn Jones for taking so much of her time to edit this book, for Father Ted Colleton's spiritual counsel; Dr. Vern Isaac for the medical input; Dr. Bernharda Meyers for sharing her medical library; Jack Kiervin's wisdom and for believing in me; James Paterson for his artwork; Katie Yeoman for proofreading; Pam Highgate and Lynn Kofler, both RN's who did much of the medical research and Paul Broughton, my publisher.

Contents

Dedication . . . . *v*

Acknowledgments . . . . *vi*

Introduction . . . . *ix*

1. Sex: Should I or Shouldn't I? *1*

2. Birth Control:
   What You Really Need to Know! *9*

3. Men: For Your Eyes Only *19*

4. Consequences of Sex Outside of Marriage. *29*

5. How Far is Too Far? *43*

6. Creative Dating *51*

7. The Love Test *63*

8. The Greatest Gift of All *77*

9. Benefits of Waiting Until Marriage *83*

10. Secondary Virginity *93*

11. What Do I Do With My Broken Heart?. . . . *97*

12. Questions Most Asked by Teens *105*
    Hot Lines for the Nineties *115*

13. Warning: Don't Read, It's Religious! *127*

    Appendix I
    Birth Control *138*

    Appendix II
    Character Identity Determination *159*

    Appendix III
    Studies on Sexual Activity,
    Chastity and Divorce *160*

    Directory *170*

    Books to Read *173*

    Birth Control Bibliography *175*

    Footnotes *181*

Introduction

People ask me how I got started as a chastity counsellor and speaker since my background is business administration and computer programming, certainly worlds apart!

If you are interested in a detailed story of how that change took place, you might find chapter 13 of interest. Suffice it to say that because of my own need for answers, together with countless singles across the country, I decided to research this area until I was satisfied with the answers I needed to hang on to my hormones until marriage. I am still single and know from first hand experience the difficulty of living a chaste life in our sex saturated society.

I have received invitations to speak about chastity from countries around the world. Speaking at schools, churches, youth groups and conferences has become a full time occupation. It is wonderful to realize that **chastity** really is an **"idea whose time has come!"**

Hang on to your hormones, don't let go
Someone's going to stomp on them, don't you know

AIDS, disease, abortion is part of the sex game
Young or rich don't matter, death knows your name
Herpes, warts and cancer; crabs and even lice
Honey, you drop your pants, you pay the price

Hang on to your hormones, why throw them away
Someone's gonna stomp on them, they want to play

We are the future, chastity leads the way
We're not going to do it, til our wedding day
Even if you'd had sex before, its not too late
Secondary virginity is the 90s way to date

Sooooo, Hang on to your hormones, save all this fun
Celebrate sex in marriage with your loved one!

Chapter 1

Sex: Should I Or Shouldn't I?

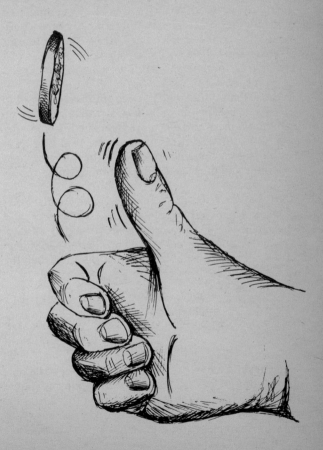

The problem with hard decisions is not making them but learning to live with the consequences.

According to most media, sex has become the national indoor sport of North America. Before we ever date, we should have decided logically and rationally what we are going to do about our hormones. Are we going to wait until marriage before becoming sexually active or will some other factor determine this very important experience of our lives.

Because I am not sexually active and have decided to wait until marriage, many guys won't date me. Others think I am a prize and are more interested in a scoring opportunity than getting to know the real me. I am invisible to them. However there are other guys to whom I am visible and they want to spend time getting to know the real me.

This really started me thinking. Do you realize that the average married couple spends roughly one and a quarter hours (75 minutes) a week in sexual activity[1] which is about twice a week! That's it. There are 168 hours in a week. Putting sex at 2 hr. (which is higher than the average!) we have:

Work	40	
Sleep	56	
Eat	5	
Total	103	hours

That means there are still 65 hours in the week available to developing relationships. All I am denying anyone is two hours a week. Any person can give another two hours of sex a week, but if a person really likes me and wants to get to know me, he needs to hang around with me. Sex should never be the deciding factor in a relationship. Many marriages break up because the 65 available hours have never been developed to their full potential prior to marriage, due to an emphasis on planning and experiencing the sexual aspect of the relationship. All married couples have occasional fights. They still work and sleep. The two hours of sex a week definitely goes until they make up. That is why the friendship part of any relationship is of the utmost importance.

Another way of looking at this big question is by evaluating how much of my life will account for this activity and what will be the consequences. Newsweek Magazine in Jan. of 1989 listed the amount of time spent over a lifetime doing various activities as follows:

Reading junk mail	8 mths.
Stopping at red lights	6 mths.
Eating	6 yrs.
Housework	4 yrs.
Talking on the telephone	2 yrs.
Looking for lost objects	1 yr.

I added	TV	8 yrs.	(Stats Can.)
	sleep	25 yrs.	(8 hrs./day)
	work	11 yrs.	
	Sex	7 mths.	

(2 x 52 weeks x 50 yrs. married = 5200 hours
divided by 24 = 215 days divided by 30 =
7 months and 5 days!

Over a lifetime we probably spend more time looking for lost objects than we do in sexual activity!

If a person lives an average life span of 75 years and the average age of marriage is 25, then there are potentially 50 years in the married state. 97%[2] of today's teens desire marriage, do not want divorce and believe that faithfulness in marriage is important. Therefore it makes sense to look very seriously at what makes a good marriage.

The divorce rate in Canada is over 40%. The highest divorce rate is experienced by couples who choose to live together before marriage (80% higher than those who did not live together first).[3] Those who marry because the woman is pregnant experience a divorce rate of 76%.[4]

Couples who are married in a church and continue to regularly attend church have a 1 in 50 divorce rate (2%). Of couples who are married in a church, continue to attend church and have a family *prayer life at home* only 1 in 1,105 are divorced (.09%) as reported by the 1981 US census.

Two virgins or secondary virgins experience a divorce rate of no higher than 3% from all the studies that I have been able to find. See Appendix III.

In June 1985, **Psychology Today** published the results of a survey. They asked couples married 25 years or more, "What keeps your marriage going?"

The responses were:

1. **My spouse is my best friend.**
2. I like my spouse as a person.
3. Marriage is a long term commitment.
4. Marriage is sacred.
5. We agree on aims and goals.
6. My spouse has grown more interesting.
7. I want the relationship to succeed.
8. An enduring marriage is important to social stability.
9. We laugh together.
10. I am proud of my spouse's achievements.
11. We agree on a philosophy of life.
12. We agree about our sex life.
13. We agree on how and how often to show affection.
14. I confide in my spouse.
15. We share outside hobbies and interests.

When I was a teenager, I found sex got in the way of knowing if I really loved the guy because sexual intimacy felt so good most of the time. I usually got involved with the guy before I really knew him. All of a sudden, I would realize that I did not like this guy as much as I thought I did, *but* because we were already sexually involved, I felt obligated to continue the relationship. I hoped I could change him.

When that didn't work, I accepted the relationship until there was a big problem that wouldn't go away. I was pregnant!

To make this major decision, write down the advantages gained by becoming sexually active before marriage and the possible disadvantages.

Advantages To Sex Before Marriage

_____

_____

_____

_____

_____

Disadvantages To Sex Before Marriage

_____

_____

_____

_____

_____

_____

_____

_____

_____

_____

_____

_____

If you didn't fill out most of the lines listed for disadvantages, please read chapter 4.

Now let's look at the "Advantages of waiting until marriage" and "The disadvantages of waiting".

Disadvantages of Waiting

_____

_____

_____

_____

_____

Advantages of Waiting

_____

_____

_____

_____

_____

_____

_____

_____

_____

_____

_____

_____

If you haven't filled out most of the lines, then please read chapters 8 & 9 very carefully before making your final decision.

Honeymoon Virgins

I travelled across Canada interviewing couples that had chosen to wait until marriage before being sexually active. Then I produced a video called "Chastity: A Question of Choice".

Every couple except one stated that trying to hold on to their hormones until marriage was the most difficult part of their relationship. One couple had to break up for a period of three months because they started going too far and felt they were getting dangerously close to going all the way. The three month breakup helped them to regain their perspective and strengthened their commitment to wait until marriage.

Life is filled with decisions, and few have so much effect on your future as the decision to have or not have sex before marriage. If you are unmarried, you owe it to yourself — and to your future husband or wife — to read this book and think it out for yourself, rather than letting others pressure you.

Chapter 2

Birth Control:
What You Really Need To Know!

We need to consider the morality of birth control as well as the physical aspect. Many religions still believe that artificial contraceptives are immoral. The IUD and every combination of birth control pill have the potential to cause an early abortion, making these particular types of contraceptives contrary to the moral application of life.

1. *All methods of contraceptive work better for married people.* Married couples are far more successful using birth control than singles. The Canadian "Report on Oral Contraceptives, 1985" states on page 19, "Teenagers present a special problem. They are sporadic rather than consistent contraceptive users". Studies done by Planned Parenthood have confirmed this government report. Teens are also at their peak of fertility which increases the risk of pregnancy.

2. *Virgins can get pregnant!* How, you ask, if they are not sexually active? The important thing to remember is that it is not the act of intercourse that makes one pregnant. It is the joining of a sperm with the egg. If any sperm are deposited near the vagina and fertility mucus is present, that is close enough for sperm to travel to the egg. One does not have to break the hymen (the thin membrane that partially covers the vaginal opening) to become pregnant.

3. *You can get pregnant the first time.* Pregnancy has nothing to do with experience but has everything to do with a woman being fertile or ovulating.

4. *You can get pregnant before you start your first menstrual cycle.* This is true because a woman or teen will ovulate first and then approximately two weeks later, she will experience menarche or her first period.

5. *You can get pregnant during the menstrual phase of your cycle.* It has been known to happen particularly if a woman misreads the signs. There is no guarantee that you can never get pregnant during your period. There is always a risk.

6. *You can get pregnant on the pill.* There are 23 known drugs that may reduce the effectiveness of the pill. Studies recommend that other methods of contraceptive be used while on the following drugs:

Anticonvulsants
   Phenobarbital
   Carbamazepine
   Ethosuximide
   Phenytoin
   Primidone

Antibiotics
   Ampicillin
   Penicillin
   Griseofulvin
   Chloramphenicol
   Metronidazole
   Neomycin
   Nitrofurantoin
   Sulfonamides
   Tetracycline
   Rifampicin

Sedatives, Hypnotics, Tranquilizers
   Benzodiazepines
   Barbiturates
   Chloral Hydrate
   Glutethimide
   Meprobamate

Antacids
  All Varieties

Other Drugs (Possible Problems)
  Phenylbutazone
  Antihistamines
  Analgesics
  Antimigrane Preparations

Note: Use another method of contraceptive or use another drug. (See page 116-117 of "Managing Contraceptive Pill Patients" by Richard P. Dickey, M.D., PhD) These findings are verified in "The Report on Oral Contraceptives, 1985" by the Committee on Reproductive Physiology to the Health Protection Branch, Health and Welfare Canada, 1985.

Drugs Whose Action May Be Modified
By Oral Contraceptives
  Aminocaproic Acid
  Anticoagulants (all)
  Anticonvulsants (all)
  Antidiabetic Agents
    Insulin
    Oral Hypoglycemic agents
  Antihypertensive Agents
    Guanethidine
    Methyldopa
  Tricyclic Antidepressants
    Clomipramine
    Possibly others
  Betamimetic Agents
    Isoproterenol
  Beta Blocking Agents
    Metoprolol

Phenothiazine Tranquilizers
    Phenothiazines (all)
    Reserpine and similar drugs
Sedatives and Hypnotics
    Chlordiazepoxide
    Lorazepam
    Oxazepam
    Diazepam

Note: Recommendation was to either change the dosage of the pill while on the above drugs, or to stop taking the pill while on these drugs and use another method of contraceptive while on the above medications, or change the medications.

7. *Teens have the highest pregnancy rate in every category of birth control.* Married couples experienced the highest effective rates compared to teens and singles in their twenties. Look at the following study as reported by William R. Grady, Mark D. Hayward, and Junichi Yagi, "Contraceptive Failure in the United States: Estimates for the 1982 National Survey of Family Growth", Family Planning Perspectives 18:5 (New York: Alan Guttmacher Institute, Sept/Oct, 1986), p. 204.

	Contraceptive Failure	
	Singles Under 18	**Singles Over 18**
Pill	11%	6%
Diaphragm	32%	23%
IUD	11%	5%
Condoms	18%	11%
Spermicides	34%	19%
No Method	63%	45%

The figures show that a teen under the age of 18 using the pill has an 11% chance of getting pregnant. It means of every 100 women using the pill 11 got pregnant in one year. If the 100 single woman using the pill were over the age of 18 the number of pregnancies would be 6.

8. *Couples with no intention of having another child have always had better results from any method than those who wished only to space births.*[1]

Figures in the table below reflect the number of actual pregnancies in one year out of 100 women using each method.

	No More Children	More
Pill	4	7
IUD	5	15
Condom	10	21
Diaphragm	17	25
Foam	22	36

9. *Natural Family Planning is the most effective form of avoiding pregnancy.* The World Health Organization states that NFP is 98.5% effective in avoiding pregnancy. This method can also be used to achieve a pregnancy. This is *not* the Rhythm Method which was used years ago. Just as there are signs of spring time, so are there signs of fertility which can be easily identified once taught how to read these signs.

Check for the nearest Natural Family Planning Centre in your local Yellow Pages. Authors Harvey & Marilyn Diamond also promote Natural Family Planning in their national bestseller "Fit For Life II: Living Health". NFP teaches every woman, no matter the irregularity of her cycle, to understand when her body is ovulating so she can abstain from sexual activity during that time. It is totally healthy and encourages honest communication between couples. Note however, that this method records a lower effective rate for teens and singles.

10. *Intercourse, even with a condom, with a person known to be infected with the HIV virus (which causes AIDS) is so dangerous anyone in such a situation should "consider alternative methods of expressing physical intimacy".* That is a statement from a U.S. Public Health Service Task Force made up of representatives from the Food and Drug Administration (FDA), the Centers for Disease Control (CDC), and the National Institute for Health (NIH). The study group was convened in December 1988 by then Surgeon General C. Everett Koop to review the latest condom research data, and this warning was issued on February 17, 1989. Do you understand what this means? Advertising and programs that promote condoms as safe do not have the support of these most respected agencies. Yet we are still being told that condoms provide safe sex.

The pores of the latex condom can be measued, and the diameters of viruses can be measured also. The natural channels in condom rubber measure 5 microns while the measurement of an HIV/AIDS virus is from .1 to .3 microns. The virus can pass through the molecular structure of a condom that is supposedly without defect!

Would you trust your life with such a product?

11. *All the sperm required to repopulate the entire world fit inside an aspirin tablet!* As reported by Dr. Niels Laurersen, page 61 of his book "It's Your Body". That is 5 billion sperm. 85,000 sperm can 'dance' on the size of a dot or 230 million HIV virus on the same size dot.

12. *Sperm are not just released at orgasm.* Men produce an average of 50 million sperm a day. During one sexual encounter, it is possible for a man to pass anywhere from 200 million to 500 million sperm in a race to reach one egg. During a woman's ovulation, she produces a special mucus that transports the sperm to the egg. It is like a slippery highway right to the egg. Sperm can be found in urine and lubricating fluids during arousal. If any contact is made anywhere in the vaginal area of a fertile woman, it is very possible that she could become pregnant. By the time the condom is used, it may be too late!

13. *Please look at Appendix I for detailed information on all forms of birth control.* It is very serious for women because their fertility could be compromised by many of the birth control methods that are commonly promoted. Women never get a new set of ovaries. All the eggs a woman will ever have in her lifetime are with her at birth.
  Damage to the ovaries or to the eggs reduces chances of successful childbearing. It is interesting that North America has the highest infertility rate in the world. Part of that is due to the IUD, the Pill, and abortions. Also women who choose to have children later in life are not as fertile. The peak fertility time for women is during their teen years, which could also explain why teens have the highest pregnancy rates of any age category.

14. *Please look at the Bibliography* if you decide to investigate this issue any further. Don't just accept what I am telling you. Check it out for yourself. That means don't believe any one source. Research; get as many facts as possible.

15. *Not all sexually transmitted diseases (STD'S) are transmitted sexually.* Some are skin to skin contact such as Human Papilloma Virus (HPV) (which has recently been

closely linked with genital tract cancers), and the herpes simplex virus. They are frequently found in vulva, clitoris, anal and groin areas. One would need to wear a full rubber diaper to have any impact on these viruses. If the HIV virus is found in the semen, then it is most definitely found in the blood and other body fluids. Any open sores or little cuts could be enough to transmit the virus to the uninfected partner.

16. *Once a person is infected with the HIV virus, he/she is infected for LIFE.* Remember when you have sex with someone, you are sleeping with all the partners he/she ever had before, as well as all the partners they ever had.

Chapter 3

Men: For Your Eyes Only

This chapter has been the most difficult for me to write. It was also the last chapter I wrote for this book. I felt it was very important for men to understand women a little better.

This chapter is from my heart to your heart. I would like to be **understood** by you and to understand you as well. That is why this chapter is **for your eyes only.** I had to write it as if there were no women around, otherwise my thoughts became more muddled.

Guys, you are special. I want you to know that. You are uniquely different from us. If we could only stop competing against each other and start complimenting each other, the world would surely be a fantastic place for everyone. We have equal value as being part of the human race but we are different.

I think men have been given a bum rap in so many areas. Yes, you have made a lot of mistakes in history. You've exploited women and made them objects or property. This is one of the main reasons that the women's movement has gained such momentum.

Today, I think we have taken it almost too far. We blame you for all our woes. For that I am truly sorry. Sorry because I was part of that movement that went way beyond true equal rights. Forgive me! Neither men or women have the right to push their side more than the other.

We call you cold, callous, unloving, unfeeling, and insensitive. Most single families are headed by women. It's hard to think differently of you men when so many young women I counsel at our centre come in pregnant and 79% of the time, the guy abandons her. That's hard, especially because the reason for the breakup has nothing to do with the person this woman is but has everything to do with being sexually active. Infatuation or so called "chemistry" goes right down the drain. It happened to me.

One minute I was loved and adored; the next minute, I was rejected. I hadn't changed. Reality was still the same.

I was the same personality as before the knowledge of pregnancy. My body hadn't even changed in size. But now I had a condition; I was pregnant and I found that I wasn't loved anymore. I was rejected. Because of this I was very angry. After the abortion, I left the guy. I hated him and I guess I had a lot of anger at guys in general.

Your physical attraction to women actually gets in the way of finding a psychologically compatible life partner. Men, you are generally body, mind and soul (heart) while women are heart, body and mind. In other words, women tend to be emotional first, then give of themselves physically. Men, you give of your body long before you give of your emotions. You may never emotionally love a woman yet you could very easily have a sexual relationship with her.

It's easier for guys to go to prostitutes because you really can love one woman while having sex with another. You can separate love from sex. Women generally see sex as an expression of love or use sex to get love.

You look at a gorgeous woman, and you say "Wow, I want her". In your mind you think she can make you happy. You want to possess her. You have no idea what type of personality she is. If she is beautiful on the outside, you believe that she couldn't be anything but beautiful on the inside. You don't know what kind of person she is. As a matter of fact you may love her more as long as she keeps her mouth closed! Why? You project your idea of a woman into that body and you love your idea. It's not that you really love the very heart and soul that are contained in the beautiful body.

It's interesting that during war time, when soldiers married women of other cultures, as long as neither one spoke the other's language, they got along beautifully. But as soon as they started to communicate in the same language, the marriages became a disaster. Most broke up. The reason was that each was in love with love and felt it would be packaged a certain way. There was obviously a great physical attraction for each other. This just proves how dangerous it is to make decisions on a physical level. If no emotional bonding takes place, the relationship is doomed to failure. For some of the couples, getting to really know each other actually strengthened the relationship, but that was the minority.

We are three parts naturally: mind, body and soul. When I say mind, I'm not just talking about the mass of information we store in our brain. I am talking about the sum total of all our past experiences. Each one has a higher level rapport. The physical is the lowest level of communication. Two people could meet and in 5 minutes or less be sexually united. Many people complain that a one night stand was not sexually stimulating or enjoyable because there was no meeting of the minds.

The next level of relating for men is the mind or logical realm, then the emotional. That's why marriages that are based on a solid friendship have the highest success rate for happiness. If sex is introduced prematurely, the growth in the other areas will become stunted. The sexual part is so overpowering, it gets in the way of heightening the level of intimacy through the friendship level.

The highest level of relating is spiritually. I'm sure you have heard about soul mates. Few couples ever really come to that point of loving beyond the natural realm, of loving totally, unconditionally with full knowledge of the other person's faults. That has got to be the greatest.

Let me explain it another way. We have one dimensional, two dimensional, and three dimensional objects. A one dimensional object **never** contains a two dimensional or three dimensional one. Now a two dimensional also includes the one dimensional but it has no three dimensional aspects. The three dimensional object also contains within it two dimensional and one dimensional objects.

I equate the physical with the first dimension; logic with the second dimension and the emotions with the third dimension.

For relationships to be three dimensional, one has to become a three dimensional being before starting to court or date. You have to learn how to be that kind of person. Once you learn how to be fully real and honest with yourself and others, then you are ready to begin to develop emotionally fulfilling relationships. The physical must not be introduced too soon.

The spiritual plain is the fourth dimension of self. This cannot be measured in the same way as one, two or three dimensional objects. The fourth dimension is parallel to quantum physics.

Physical man is sexually attracted to women. Logic tells him that in order to have sex with woman, he must manipulate the relationship, therefore he uses loving words, romance, and promises of commitment to get her. It's a goal, a challenge. That's how it starts. It may never be done on a conscious level because of the powerful force of physical attraction. The relationship may stay that way for ever or move into higher level emotional intimacy. Physical intimacy deceives many people into believing they have accomplished emotional intimacy. All components of self must participate in the selection of a partner in order for the relationship to be a success.

There is a fourth dimension to relationships and that takes a quantum leap to achieve. That is the spiritual side of us. Each person has a spirit whether or not one wants to believe it. It's sad to marry someone who is your spiritual opposite.

The man I was engaged to was a dear friend before I ever started dating him. Perhaps that was why we were planning to get married. We had no expectations of each other. I never dreamed I would ever date this guy so I never tried to impress him. I was myself and he was himself. When we started dating our relationship grew in reality and was strengthened as the years went by. When I experienced my spiritual conversion, my fiancé was shocked and totally negative about it. Although we were good physically and emotionally together, we were not spiritually compatible at all. Our relationship immediately ended two months before our planned wedding day. As a matter of fact we broke up on the original date we had planned to marry, Oct. 13, 1981!

I have observed that sex gets in the way of love. Sex gets in the way of loving one another and sex gets in the way of loving God when it is pursued outside of marriage.

So how does one take that quantum leap into relationships? I have never heard it said better than by Bill Russell, the famous Boston Celtics basketball player who described how he reached metaphysical heights in his book *Second Wind: The Memoirs of an Opinionated Man".*

"Every so often a Celtic game would heat up so that it became more than a physical or even mental game and would be magical. That feeling is difficult to describe, and I certainly never talked about it when I was playing. When it happened, I could feel my play rise to a new level. It came rarely, and would last anywhere from five minutes to a whole quarter or more. Three or four players were not enough to get it going. It would surround not only me and the other Celtics, but also the players on the other team, and even the referees.

At that special level, all sorts of odd things happened. The game would be in a white heat of competition, and yet somehow I wouldn't feel competitive — which is a miracle in itself. I'd be putting out the maximum effort, straining, coughing up parts of my lungs as we ran and yet never feel the pain. The game would move so quickly that every fake, cut and pass would be surprising and yet nothing could surprise me. It was almost as if we were playing in slow motion. During these spells, I could almost sense how the next play would develop and where the next shot would be taken. Even before the other team brought the ball in bounds, I could feel it so keenly that I'd want to shout to my teammates, "It's coming there!" — except that I knew everything would change if I did. My premonitions would be consistantly correct, and I always felt then that I not only knew all the Celtics by heart, but also all the opposing players, and that they all knew me. There have been many times in my career when I felt moved or joyful but these were the moments when I had chills pulsing up and down my spine".

That's the quantum leap I'm talking about but apply it to a relationship between the opposite sexes. What a wonder that would be.

It's easy to love with your genitals but to love with your mind, your heart, your spirit takes real effort. It's easy to kiss with your lips but can you kiss with your eyes? Can you reach down into the innermost depths of who you are and touch the very core of another soul and not run? It's scary but worth the risk. To know that the woman you are with loves you unconditionally and accepts you and for you to love her the same way back is so exhilarating and freeing.

It's harder for men to reach this level of intimacy due to cultural conditioning as well as psychological makeup, but your capacity to love a woman is far greater than any woman's love. Sure women fall in love easier and they bounce back after a broken heart a lot easier too. When you love a woman mind, body and soul and she breaks your heart, you have a much harder time bouncing back. The suicide rate among teenage guys is 5-6 times higher than teenage girls and three times higher for men over women.

Pornography is one of the quickest ways to destroy a man's ability to love a woman in all dimensions. At best, pornography is surface sex, treating women as sex objects. It becomes very addictive because the focus is on the imagination and the orgasm rather than on the journey. Women enjoy foreplay and need to feel that they are loved to the very core of their being. Pornography causes problems in the bedroom with the husband experiencing premature ejaculation and temporary impotency with spouse while still enjoying porn.

Judith A. Reisman, PhD wrote in her book, "Soft Porn Plays Hardball", "Every second, 100 million messages bombard the brain carrying information from the body's senses". Only a few of these are heeded by the conscious mind. Only the most important — or exciting-sense information gets through. This suggests why pornography has such an impact on people — young and old. When one reaches a state of emotional arousal faster than the body can rally its adaptive reactions, a form of stress follows. Briefly, the male body is designed to respond — or adapt — to blatant female coital signals by engaging in sexual intercourse. Anything which increases sexual stress (e.g. sexual signal, sexual shame, sexual fear) triggers known physiological mechanisms. In an instant, anxiety mobilizes the body into a chain reaction of defenses with a single aim: to put the body in top physical condition to cope with the emergency. Chemicals seep into the pituitary gland, releasing a stress hormone known as adreno-corticotropic hormone (acth). Scores of other neuro-chemicals are sped into action as well, notably adrenaline and noradrenaline. The bronchial tubes relax and open for deeper breathing. Blood sugar is increased for maximum energy. The heart beats faster and contracts strongly; stress will arouse (all) vital organs...

Moreover, the central nervous system (CNS) treats sexual or violent stimuli nondiscriminatively. In response to violent or sexual stimuli, males and females create "brain chemicals" including adrenaline, a kind of naturally produced morphine. In addition, males produce testosterone, a steroid that fuels both creative energy (sex) and destructive energy (violence). (Females produce estrogen and a minute amount of testosterone. Estrogen does not generate aggressiveness).[1]

Exposure to pornography generally increases one's heart rate, respiration, blood pressure, and the like. It is dangerous to refer to this aroused state as 'sexual drive', however, since it will tend to include a mixture of emotions such as *fear, anger,* and *shame.*

Intensity of arousal (in most, if not all cases) increases in proportion to one's level of stress...responding to a "sex" cue experienced in a state of fear, anger or shame should trigger — temporarily — a "higher" arousal state than would be "normal"; no longer new, conjugal love and trust.

That is the dangerous problem of pornography: it becomes so addictive. There is no satisfaction level in sight. After awhile the body adjusts to the material. At the point where there is no longer any arousal from the magazine, a level of desensitization (or habituation) has generally been reached. There are no measurable vital signs between the reading of "Time Magazine" and viewing "Playboy". When the brain adapts to a novel sensation, arousal is dramatically reduced. It is then necessary to seek out more exciting experiences (i.e. more hostile, violent, shameful pornography) in order to satisfy the desire for that "high".

Pornography is addictive and causes many problems in marriage. A young woman wrote Ann Landers complaining that her husband could not make love to her until he had looked at some pornographic material first. Is he really making love to his wife or just using her body to finish what was started in his mind?

Also remember that the average married couple experience sexual relations 2 — 3 times per week. Masturbation beyond the above amount will no doubt lead to some dissatisfaction to one or both partners.

If women are seen only as sex objects, then to love a woman in all dimensions is near impossible. You may even really love your woman or spouse but find yourself unable to express your love in the sex act. Because women see sex as an expression of their emotional love, they can find it very difficult to understand that you really love even though you have little desire for your spouse sexually.

Remember that at whatever level you enter into in the relationship, you will never know when you have passed to a higher or more intimate level until you either:

Break up
She gets pregnant
You get married

The physical intimacy can easily be confused with emotional or spiritual intimacy. Only after a life changing event has taken place, will you know your own heart. How many movies have you seen where the guy only knew how much he loved the woman after they broke up?

That is why it is so important to start a relationship at the highest level of intimacy...spiritual, then logically rule the emotions and then in marriage release the physical level to express all the other types of love to your spouse.

I desire with all my heart to connect to my husband mind, body, and soul. To be as soul mates. I believe that you too, desire such a relationship but you have been pressured into being other than who you really are.

So my friend, seek out your spiritual identity. Search your heart to find your emotional personality. Use your logic and talents to find your destiny. Climb your mountains, conquer those glacier covered peaks, follow the sun, dream your dreams, develop friendships closer than those with your own brother or sister! But hang on to all your passion, your physical desires for your soul mate. Learn who you are. Redirect your physical or one dimensional energies into taking a quantum leap into fourth dimensional living.

Then, somewhere in time, you will meet your mate and in marriage consummate your vows sexually and take a quantum leap of love together, never to be the same again!

Chapter 4

Consequences of Sex Outside of Marriage

"A driver's licence is more difficult to obtain than a marriage licence!"

When you ask yourself if you are ready for a sexual relationship as a single person, please consider the following information. Think through very carefully what you would do if you or your partner got pregnant. Despite birth control, pregnancy is still a *very possible outcome!*

Each year over 600,000 teens get pregnant in USA and 50,000 in Canada. Almost half will get abortions. Half of the single moms will drop out of school.

Remember, a lot of these teens were using some form of contraceptives. My boyfriend and I were using both a condom and foam when I got pregnant. The female is always the one who gets pregnant!

Any of the following choices are very difficult when you are not emotionally, physically or financially prepared to raise a child.

Pregnancy

When a couple is married, pregnancy can certainly be an exciting experience as both parents look forward to the birth of their baby. Without marriage, the news of pregnancy is usually not received with joy by either partner, especially the young man. Many men leave a relationship at this point, particularly if the woman decides to go through with the pregnancy. Sometimes guilt will bring the couple together in marriage. However, the divorce rate among couples pregnant at the altar is 76%.[1]

Abortion

Abortion is another choice when a woman is single and pregnant. Over 92% of abortions are done by a method called Suction D & C, usually between the eighth and twelfth week of gestation.

Fact: 18 days after conception, the heartbeat of the fetus (Latin for "young one") can be detected.

Fact: At 6 weeks, the young one moves in the womb actually swimming the backstroke. Brain waves are present.

Fact: At 8 weeks, the young one grabs, squints, moves freely. His or her lips and palms are sensitive to gentle touch.

Fact: By 12 weeks, all internal organs are present and functioning. The young one breathes, swallows, digests and urinates and is very sensitive to heat and pain.

Possible Consequences of Abortion:
   Sexual dysfunction
   Lower self-esteem
   Relationship breaks up (70%)

There are over 32 recorded physical complications which can occur as a result of abortion. These include:

   Retained products of conception
   Rupture of the uterus
   Perforation of the bladder
   Perforation of the bowel
   Myocardial infarction
   Kidney damage and loss
   Torn intestines
   Salt poisoning
   Milk secretion
   Loss of sleep
   Vomiting
   Spleen removal
   Water intoxication
   Increase of ectopic pregnancies in future
   Damage to cervix
   Hemorrhage
   Infection

Perforation of the uterus
Sterility
Complications of future pregnancies
Increased number of miscarriages
Fallopian tube damage
Dysmenorrhea
Endometritis
Amenorrhea
Complicated labour if late abortion
Congenital handicap
Developmental problems
Low birthweight
Placenta previa
Perinatal mortality increase
Risk of central nervous system damage
Rh blood disease

There are over 33 recorded psychological manifestations
of Post Abortion Syndrome.
These include:

Severe depression
Anniversary syndrome
Suicidal thoughts
Substance abuse
Nightmares and/or hallucinations
Phantom pregnancies
Guilt
Unresolved grieving
Self-hatred
Anguish
Numbness
Regret
Shock
Family Feticidal Syndrome
Desire to end relationship with partner

Feelings of helplessness
Intense interest in babies
Looking at babies connects to abortion
Preoccupation with would be birthdate
Preoccupation with death
Misdirected anger
Self destructive behavior
Repeat abortions
Hatred towards any one connected with abortion
Inability to sustain an intimate relationship

Adoption

Adoption is never easy. A childless couple receives a priceless gift. It takes incredible courage and sacrificial love to release a child for adoption.

If you happen to be adopted, please know that your mother loves you very much. If she didn't, she simply would have done what I did...get an abortion. But she stayed pregnant just for you.

She may have had to drop out of school for awhile or even leave home. She got fat and carries the stretch marks of your delivery for the rest of her life. That's love.

When your mom found out she was pregnant, she did not reject her baby, she rejected her circumstances. She honestly believed that her circumstances were not the most loving ones to raise you in so she gave you to another family to love, support and raise in an environment that was only a dream to her.

In Ontario in 1987, there were over 30,000 abortions and only 766 babies were released for adoption. Many women like me thought it was easier to abort than to adopt. Looking back over my life, I know I made the wrong choice. Adoption takes great love and courage.

Each province and state controls adoption procedures. Most agencies now allow more control to the birthmother than ever before. If she wants to choose the adopting parents, she may do so. If she wants to leave it up to the professionals, they can make the decision. They will do whatever is best for the surrendering mother and her baby. She may even get pictures and letters from the family if that is agreed on before the adoption papers are signed. Confidentiality is assured.

Single Parenting

Single parenting is not easy if a young girl has no support from family or friends or the father. She often drops out of school and ends up on mother's allowance or welfare.

Please check your local community information centre or call us to find out what kind of support is available in your community. With proper assistance, one can overcome the odds.

Statistics Canada reported that over 46,000 teens got pregnant during 1991. Over 15,000 had abortions. 50% of them will never complete high school.

Possible Consequences of Single Parenting:
    Drop out of school
    Boyfriend leaves
    Early marriage
    Higher risk for child abuse
    Higher risk for later divorce
    Heavy financial burdens
    Fulltime work if left to raise child alone
    Try to survive on welfare

Marriage

As mentiond earlier, when a couple chooses to marry because of a pregnancy, the divorce rate is 76%.

If marriage was planned before the knowledge of pregnancy, there is a better chance of a successful marriage. Remember that teen marriages have a three times higher divorce rate than the national average according to the Community Task Force.

What About The Guy?

Guys can suffer too, but in a different way. They don't get pregnant. No man can be forced under any circumstances to marry the woman **but** if the woman chooses to name him as the father and to pursue financial support, the legal system will stand on the side of the child and demand payment. It doesn't matter if you love her or not.

Child support payments can range anywhere from $200.00 to $1,200.00 a month depending on the financial standing or the potential earning power of the man. However, in the USA, many states work on a fixed rate per child.

If the man wants the baby and the woman does not, the highest courts in the land still say that the decision is up to the woman. She can say "It's my body and I do what I want with my body!" It's totally the woman's decision whether or not she gets and abortion. The man has no say. It's not fair but that is the reality at this time.

We counselled in a situation where the young lady had promised to have an abortion if she got pregnant, but when she did get pregnant, she told the man that she had changed her mind and could not go through with an abortion. They were living together. She chose to keep the baby and the man left her. Because they had been living together, she was able to successfully charge him with child support. It did not matter what she had previously said.

In another case, the young lady told the guy to leave her alone, as her parents were going to help her if she broke up with him. He was relieved, but 5 years later she was seeking child support from him because she had changed her mind!

We have also counselled men who have suffered feelings of tremendous loss because of their lack of control in the situation. The youngest father we counselled was 14 years old.

Sexually Transmitted Disease

Two virgins who marry do not get sexually transmitted diseases (STDs). This happens because of previous sexual contact. It takes only one of the partners to have had other sexual contacts to spread the disease. Most STDs can be readily treated if caught in the early stages. But sterility is a common consequence, especially for women. Now that we have the HIV virus, death is also a definite possible consequence. Quite a price to pay for a few moments of pleasure!

The most heartbreaking situations I have counselled are those teens who contracted the AIDS virus (HIV) the very first time they were sexually active. One sexual encounter has the power to create life through pregnancy and now one sexual encounter has the power to destroy life through AIDS.

Clearly any STD is undesirable but people often get more than one infection at a time. The ultimate result almost always damages women to a much greater degree than men because it can destroy her ability to have children or be passed on to her future children when they are being born.

There is *No Safe Sex* only *Slightly Safer Sex.* The only safe sex is no sex until marriage and both partners virgins. The next best thing is to *Stop* sexual activity now before it's too late and wait until marriage. It is not only OK to say *no, it's smart!*

Before 1960, there were only 5 known sexually transmitted diseases. Now there are over 30 different kinds of STDs and the killer is AIDS.

For detailed information about STDs please call your doctor.

Loss of Reputation

What are girls who have sex before marriage called? I travel from Newfoundland to California and girls **always** get the same names: slut, whore, easy, bitch, etc. I think you get the picture. Guys get good names. Stud, cool, macho, etc. This is the nineties; most parents are shocked that these names and double standards still exist. Yes, they heard them in their time, but figured we are far more liberated now.

Never has a young man stood up to challenge me or the audience that girls only get called sluts after 5 guys or whatever. It has never happened!

Guys have sex outside of marriage = Stud
Girls have sex outside of marriage = Slut

There is a proverb that states "Out of the abundance of the heart, the mouth speaks". Using those words says a lot about how a person thinks. It's a putdown. Using words like slut trashes the sexual act. It also destroys self-esteem for the gal. Saying, "I'm sorry" is not enough to heal the deep wounds to self-esteem and to the relationship itself. There are often fights in marriage where nasty words are hurled at each other.

A wife when angry at her husband can't call him stud to insult him. It doesn't work! However, the husband can call his wife a slut for burning the turkey! Even after the marriage vows are made, this name can stick if the wife engaged in premarital sex.

Two virgins who marry will have many a disagreement or fight. However they have little ammunition from their past to hurt each other with and will be more likely to keep to the issue at hand.

Guilt/Depression/Lower Self-Esteem

You may tend to justify sex outside of marriage because you are really in love. You feel it will last forever. Once that first love leaves for another, rejection, hurt and pain from the broken relationship can persist for some time. Guilt can be heavy on a young guy or girl when he or she has gone all the way. What do they say to the next love of their life? What do they say to *number two?* There was never supposed to be a number two! When a person has gone all the way, it becomes very difficult to say no in the next relationship. It helps if you have made a decision to become a secondary virgin.

Please read carefully chapter 10 which is about Secondary Virginity. It is never too late. Guys use *love* or *loving words* to get sex. After the relationship is over, the guy certainly got what he wanted…sex. The gal was using *sex* for love. Gals usually end up losing a lot more than they anticipated when they go all the way.

Broken Heart

A heart may never be the same after it has been broken in a sexual relationship. Separating is never as devastating as it is when two people have given themselves totally to each other; they are naked and vulnerable. Sexual intimacy is powerful. It binds two people together like nothing else. Even the act of marriage does not bind two people intimately until the marriage vows have been consummated.

In other words until the couple have come together in sexual union, the bond is not completed. Breaking up can be unbearable to at least one of the partners, leaving that person angry, bitter and depressed.

Isolation

Once a person starts doing something that parents or friends are opposed to, the individual tends to lie and may withdraw from those relationships. Many times relationships between teens and parents disintegrate and only after the child's marriage does the relationship mend.

Years when a parent and teen should have enjoyed a very special relationship are lost forever.

Many parents support and encourage their sons and daughters to use birth control. This often puts incredible pressure on teens who are not ready to be sexually active. This can cause anger and destroy honest communication. Many teens tell me that they feel almost pressured into having sex because of the attitude of their parents.

Development of Poor Sexual Habits and Attitudes

Let's compare premarital sex to Pavlovian Conditioning. Pavlov proved that by introducing another stimulus during a normal activity of an animal, he could change the behavior of the animal. Everytime Pavlov would feed a dog, he would ring a bell. The dog would eat and hear bells ringing. Ring bell, feed dog. Ring bell and then feed the dog.

After awhile, without any food being placed near the dog, the ringing bell would cause the dog to drool and salivate. The dog could not see, taste or smell food yet it responded exactly the same way because of association. The bell ringing would activate the natural senses of the dog for eating.

The same thing can happen sexually. There are associations around the sexual act. Rape is sex but the act is violent and against a person's will, therefore making the act very disagreeable. If a person gets used to sex in the single environment, can the adjustment be made to enjoy sex as much once the couple is married?

Think about it. When a person is single, the lifestyle is carefree with little or no responsibility. Life is spontaneous and different. One may work but there is not the overriding pressure that one *has to work*. Money is spent mostly on self. Self is all one really has to care about. You can go a hundred miles to buy an ice cream cone if you feel like it.

It is much harder to do this when there is a spouse to think of or children to worry about. Put sex into that kind of environment. Sex feels good. There is no question about that. But the single life and the married life are very different.

It is no longer 'I', it is 'We'. That is totally different. There is a commitment. There are responsibilities to one's spouse. Now you *have* to work to maintain the household. There may be mortgage payments, bills, children, job pressures.

There is now far more routine in life. When you were single you didn't care if you ate breakfast or slept in on Saturdays. Now there are children who need to eat breakfast and don't want to sleep in Saturday mornings!

Do you get the picture? Sex in a single environment is carefree, fun, with little responsibility. Sex when you are married will always carry a weight of responsibility with it. People always compare sex in the single or married life. No comparison. That is why many people say sex was great when they were single and it is boring now that they are married.

According to Pavlovian conditioning they need the single lifestyle to enjoy sex because that is what they got accustomed to.

People who wait until they are married before they are sexually active have no comparison. There are now a lot more responsibilities but they have the added enjoyment of sexual experience. Sex for these couples may be exciting and soften the blow of the added pressures that married life brings: a kind of a reward.

I would rather have 50 years of good married sex than 10 years of great single sex and a downhill slide the rest of the way.

Pornography is a big problem today with over 200 monthly magazines of soft to hardcore porn. There are more pornographic magazine or video outlets than McDonalds Restaurants.

Again the same principle of Pavlovian Conditioning can create an atmosphere for men of heightened adrenaline producing stress hormones. Chapter 3 details effects of pornography on marriage.

Chapter 5

How Far Is Too Far?

"Love Is What Love Does!"

This is the *big* question. I am asked this question almost every day of my speaking tours by singles who don't want to be sexually active yet, but who want to express their affection physically. Some young women brag about being virgins, yet they have experienced everything, and I mean everything, except vaginal penetration!

This was my own big question, too. I never had this problem before I became a Christian. And I never needed an answer until I became romantically attached to a young man. Then, wow, all the sudden the passion was almost overwhelming. I started talking to all kinds of singles about how far they went as Christians. I got as many different answers as the people I asked! I read all kinds of books on the subject and only got more confused. I wanted a straight answer. Well, I got one and here's what I found.

I share my experience to help you to be better informed as you make your decision. Perhaps it won't be the same one I made, *but* you will definitely have a better understanding of the issues.

First, let's understand the question "How far is too far?" We are talking about foreplay. You know, before the play! That is the preparation for the main event. It prepares minds, hearts and bodies to receive each other in rapturous union.

First you kiss, then kiss passionately (French kiss), fondle over the clothes, fondle under the clothes and continue south until you're home. Where does one draw the line so as not to be called a tease by the guys and a sex maniac by the gals?

Progression of Sexual Arousal

Desmond Morris in his book *Pair Bonding* (pg. 43) describes the progression of sexual arousal. He talks about the first stages of arousal or attraction which happen all the time.

Eye to body
Eye to eye
Voice to voice*
Hand to hand
Arm to shoulder
Arm to waist
Face to face
Hand to head
Mouth to mouth
Hand to body
Mouth to breast
Hand to genital
Genital to genital

*Note: Teens, tell your parents I said it's OK to be on the phone talking to each other, even for long periods of time. Just keep up all your other responsibilities. It is a *very important* part of getting to know each other at a distance without the added pressures of intense emotions. Remember that men and women have different libidos (sex drives). Women are similar to 'slow cookers' and men are similar to 'microwaves'.

A man's turn-on point is eye sight while a woman's turn-on is verbal. Generally a woman can kiss passionately (neck up a storm), fondle and caress for indefinite periods of time and feel very loving, satisfied and content.

This is more difficult for a guy purely from a biological point of view. I always wondered why the girls were called teases but when I talk to girls, they call the guys perverts and sex maniacs!

Good news! I have found the answer! You have read about how many sperm a man produces every day of his life: approximately 50 million. That works out to roughly

500 sperm every second of his life! Every second of every minute of every day of every year. 500 sperm. You're reading a book: 500 sperm a second. You're playing football: 500 sperm a second. You go to church: 500 sperm a second. EXCEPT!

There is a time when man goes into mass production! And that is when he becomes turned on. This turn-on point is different for every man. Not only is it different for every man, but it can be different for the same man on different occasions.

A man's will does not control his sex drive. How many men would wish control in that area. It is his brain. The hypothalamus gland to be exact. Men (and women) are the sum total of all their past experiences. Many of those experiences have been forgotten by the conscious mind but they are *never* forgotten by the subconscious. Very little information is stored in the conscious area. This leaves lots of information in storage ready to be recalled by a simple trigger or connector. In other words, every fantasy experienced by the mind is in the subconscious. Every bodily experience is remembered in the subconscious. Every television image, every magazine article/picture is stored forever!

The brain records all the information while the couple kiss passionately. At some point, totally beyond the control of the guy, the hypothalamus gland makes a decision. It matches the passion with the past. Hypothalamus gland says "what is sperm production like?"...Groin sends the message "production is steady at 500 sperm a second". Hypothalamus commands, "Kick into overdrive!"

Production is now 500,000 sperm a second. Do you understand? Production can go from 500 sperm a second to **500,000 sperm a second**!

How can this happen? Testosterone. Men have lots of this hormone while most women have very little of it. This hormone is not only involved in a man's sex life. It is also connected to his anger life. Testosterone can be creative energy. It is necessary for sexual as well as aggressive expression. Testosterone is also destructive energy. Anger. When a man kicks into overdrive, his body has biologically prepared him to go all the way. There is also an extra rush of adrenaline.

When the woman stops abruptly and says it's time to go home, the man must put a lid on his sexual energy. But his body is prepared for maximum performance. All this energy has to go somewhere. Since the same hormone is involved in aggression and anger, it becomes very easy for the young man to divert this energy into aggressive behavior or angry behavior.

The positive way to divert this energy is to run around the block, go play squash, or go swimming.

If that doesn't happen, his energy may be directed negatively. He may become aggressive and push to go a little further, which satisfies temporarily, or push to go all the way. He may get angry and the evening will end in a vicious fight. Date rape happens a lot but can never be excused. Remember, you can always run around the block and burn off that energy! It doesn't have to be expressed sexually. There is never a point of no return. Anyone could stop if they really had to, like if your mother walked into the room! The worst that would happen is wet pants or wet dreams. No one has died from being sexually frustrated.

The turn-on point is different for every guy. A guy who is a virgin and has not exposed himself to a lot of X-rated movies or magazines can thoroughly enjoy himself as much as the woman with going part way. Both are happy and there may be no further pressure. But a guy who has a sexual history, either real or fantasized, never knows when this overdrive situation is going to occur. Maybe one evening the relationship is wonderful...no problems. The next time, the guy has looked at porn over the noon hour or has been sexually teased by other girls or has very sexual thoughts. When he sees you, it can be very different; he has a lot of problems and is not satisfied as easily.

Each man has different levels of testosterone in his system and the same man will have different levels of testosterone in his system depending on many different internal and external conditions.

Foreplay was never meant to be totally satisfying. It was meant to prepare us to go all the way. That is why French kissing is the beginning of the slippery slope. French kissing will become the pressure point to going all the way.

Married couples don't get all turned on, fondle over the clothes, under the clothes, to the waist and then say good night and roll over. As one couple told me, they don't start the preliminaries unless they plan to stick around for the main event!

I have decided that only affectionate kissing will be part of my courting experience. Affectionate kissing is very satisfying, very loving and very tender. You're not sure what affectionate kissing is? Well, you kiss your parents, you kiss a little baby. Babies are so cute and lovable, you could just kiss them forever. You're not turned on are you?

That's affectionate kissing. For me, French kissing or passionate kissing can be too much of a turn on. It's especially difficult for the guys. I'm a secondary virgin. I have a history behind me that means it doesn't take long for me to be aroused. The guys I date are also secondary virgins. It takes them even less time to get turned on. So out of respect for the way a man is created with this incredible sexual energy that can so easily turn from creative to destructive, I have decided to refrain from French kissing until I'm married. I want to save as much of me as possible for the man I marry!

I only ask that you decide for yourselves. Think it through and then make a decision. Discuss it with your partner. Find out what his/her values are. It will make the courtship a lot easier.

Remember, different values are like two levels of water. If one is higher than the other, the high level water, if able, will flow to the lower level. The person with the lower value will drag the other down. That's why I wouldn't even consider courting a person who thought it was OK to have sex before marriage because he would try to bring me down. Even a guy who thinks it's OK to go to the waist would cause me problems because he has no qualms about going beyond kissing. I do. Therefore I would only court a man who agrees with my values. Affectionate kissing.

The choice is yours.

Chapter 6

Creative Dating

"The dignity of a career is always to be measured by the seriousness of the preparation made for it. How then do we appraise marriage?"

Herbert Newton

According to the Readers Digest Great Encyclopaedic Dictionary, "to date" in reference to relationships means "to make an appointment with". "To make an appointment with". Doesn't sound very romantic or sexy, does it?

From talking with thousands of teenagers across Canada and the United States, I've learned that they "make appointments" to kiss after school or have sex during the soaps; to go to movies, go for a walk, or go out for dinner. In many cases there was not even a pre-arranged appointment. No formal commitment to meet at a specific time to do a specific thing with a specific person. Many teens tell me they only date a guy or girl after they have necked up a storm at a party. If the feelings are good, then and only then will they pair off with that person and date.

Considering that only a few hours a week will be spent in sexual activity in marriage, it seems we have the whole thing backwards. Married people act like they are single and single people act like they are married. We want to make sure we get good sex so we start there in the relationship and then work on the emotional and social and intellectual levels. The problem with that kind of thinking is that sex is only as good as the emotional, intellectual and social development of the couple is.

In most marriages, little time is devoted to these most unglamorous areas **but** they hold the secret to a successful marriage. Best friends have the best marriages.

Lovers come and go but friends are forever. If we could change the goal of dating to making friends, not lovers, we would be a lot better off.

Dating for personal pleasure only:

* Leads to potential hurts within relationship.
* Forms the basis for conflicts in marriage.
* Ignores other important relationships such as family and friends.
* Carries hurts of old relationships into the new one.

We become engrossed in the desire for a lifetime companion. We pair up and try to enjoy the privileges of marriage during our single years and when marriage does occur, we may no longer find the need to focus on winning each other's heart. The relationship begins to cool off and the husband focuses on his business or career while the wife occupies herself with career, home and children.

The couple soon encounters the inevitable conflict which results when one or both partners neglect the responsibilities of marriage to enjoy the benefits of singleness.

When we are single, we act married.
When we are married, we act single!

Another interesting fact that I have discovered in my years of being single, relating to the opposite sex and interacting with married couples is that dating definitely belongs in marriage. It is crucial to keeping romance in a marriage. Couples need to "make an appointment with" each other at least once a week to spend time alone. To "make an appointment with" the spouse keeps them connected to one another.

The most successful marriages I have known are those of couples who allow special times to be on their own, special times with their children and above all else, special times to be alone with each other. They don't use children as an excuse not to date. One couple I know has six children and has set aside Friday nights as their time together without the children. Sometimes they only had money for the baby sitter but they would leave the children and go for a long walk or a drive in the country. The point of the matter is to make time for each other. **Marriage needs dating to keep the relationship exciting and romantic.**

Now what are singles supposed to do? I believe that singles need to experience relationships in as many different settings as possible in group situations before they move to the next step of pairing off. Before any types of formal or verbal commitments are made to that one person, again the couple should have seen each other at their very worst. Anyone can handle the best we have to offer but fewer can handle the worst.

Chapter 7 helps couples understand their relationships and potential future success in possible marital bliss with our **Love Test.**

I myself do not dream about marriage. It is not a goal in life. It is a future reality. Most of us will get married at least once. The desire for marriage in the 90s is stronger than ever. That means I don't have to work at finding a mate.

Something that I must do is to work at developing friendships with both males and females in all my areas of interest. I have sports friends, work friends, beach friends, vacation friends, mountain hiking friends, church friends, chastity friends. These friends fulfill a specific need in each of our lives. We travel in our own worlds, but in a specific area, we have been bonded together by a common interest.

I have a friend in Edmonton whom I see once a year; we go backpacking in the Rockies for a week. We have very little contact with each other outside of our common interest. We have backpacked for three years now. It is a very special friendship but not one that sustains us on a daily basis.

Then there are the inner circle of friendships that may develop from the previously mentioned categories.

A person needs a network of about a dozen friends to draw on. Within that group of 12 friends, there could be three that are very close to you; and of those three one would be your very best friend. That is a healthy life. That is a very happy life.

One's life partner will probably come out of that circle of 12 people.

For a young person, especially a teen, relationships are the most difficult to judge in honesty and reality. Life is like a pendulum, going between independence and dependence. Some areas of your life are totally under your control and your unique personality will start shining forth. Other areas are still under the control or influence of parents or peers and will surely change when the environment changes or freedom is obtained.

To a teen, everything in life is very intense. Emotions are felt very strongly but everything is still new and in an experimental stage.

When I was a teen, I tried to act grown up and I thought I knew everything. Now I am grown up and realize I know very little. I made a lot of mistakes because nobody could tell me what I didn't want to believe or hear. After years of making hundreds of stupid mistakes, I learned that listening to people I respect can save me a lot of heartache.

Have you ever heard the expression that you would like to be a fly on the wall to see what a person is really like when they are not trying to impress you?

The good news is that you can watch other people and learn about the real person from a safe distance without getting involved or hurt before you know what the person is really like. One needs to go through the four seasons of a year, at a distance, to see the person in as many different settings as possible.

The following activities are designed to allow friendships to develop at a slow and safe pace and to have a great time in the process. These activities are best done in groups from 3 to 12 people. That allows for many different types of personalities to be checked out.

Dating Strategy to Postpone Sexual Involvement

These helpful tips were written by Sue Careless of Toronto.

a) *Know your date.* Don't go out alone with a complete stranger. If you do go on a blind date, be with another couple you trust completely.

b) *Date those who are like-minded.* Discuss your values with your date before things heat up. Maybe he or she doesn't want to have sex either and is just as afraid of what you would think.

c) *Set limits and stick to them.* Make your decision about chastity before you start dating. Also, make your decision about how far you intend to go before you are caught in the heat of the moment. Half the battle is making the decision.

d) *Have a plan.* Be creative; have lots to do that's really fun. Don't spend long periods of time alone together with nothing to do.

e) *Gals as well as guys should be in on the planning of where to go and what to do.* Gals should not be afraid to share the expenses of some of the dates. This will help avoid the "I owe him/her something" syndrome. Remember, you do not owe anyone anything. Friends take care of each other and don't use each other. The same principle applies with opposite sex dating.

f) *Instead of going out on single dates (in pairs) try double or even triple dating* or go somewhere as a group or party where no one is paired off. Of course this will only protect you if the group is out for fun and not sex.

g) *If the friends are sleeping around and/or are using drugs* you will have to find a new group of friends. It won't be easy, but you'll be better off in a more positive support group.

h) *In most groups there is less pressure to "get serious"* about someone. There is usually more fun and more interesting conversation! There is also more security being with others of your sex. There's usually a lot more laughter too!

i) *Dress attractively* but not provocatively, or else you will send out mixed messages and confuse your date. Remember that guys are turned on at eye sight while women generally are turned on by touch. That means it doesn't take much to get a guy turned on. Watch how women dress at parties or at the shopping mall. You can see the difference between women who dress to stir up sexual arousal in men and women who dress to be attractive. There is a big difference.

j) *Go to walk-in movies* rather than the drive-in.

k) *Think twice about restricted movies.* Don't even glance at pornography. You are setting the stage for sex if you do.

l) *Keep your clothes on.* No matter what happens and is said, the safest thing to do is to keep *all* your clothes on.

m) *Avoid your date's house* if no one else is at home. The temptation can be too great.

n) *Avoid dating at an early age.* Research done by Josh McDowell found that if a person starts dating at age 12, there is over a 90% likelihood of being sexually active by the age of 18. If you wait until you are 14 years old to start dating, the chances of being sexually active are over 60% but if you wait until age 16 before dating, the chance of being sexually active is around 19%. You greatly reduce your risk of becoming sexually active by delaying dating.

o) *Have enough money to get home on your own if necessary.* Keep a sense of your directions also, in case you have to jump out of the car. Make sure you can see a house with lights on that you can run to. Screaming usually deters most attackers.

p) *Girls should have their date meet their parents.* It usually instills more respect for the girl in the guy. This can still be done casually.

q) *Tell your parents where you're going.* If they're going out too, make sure you have their phone number. If you don't live at home tell a friend you can trust. It is an indirect way of protecting yourself "just in case".

r) *Avoid isolated spots.* You don't want date rape.

s) *Avoid drugs and alcohol.* Drugs and alcohol can impair your ability to effectively say "no" and reduce your inhibitions. Many pregnancies have occurred while the gal was under the influence. Some times she was not aware how much she had drunk but before she could get things under control, she had gone all the way. This is a sad way to lose your virginity or to get pregnant.

t) *Feel free to use or blame your parents* if you want to set certain limits: "My parents want me home by…" "My parents won't let me…" While it's good to stand on your own two feet, it some times helps to have the back-up authority of a parent.

u) *Respect the word "No".* At any point, either individual has the right to say no to physical contact. When a woman says "no" she does not mean "sweep me off my feet". When a guys says "no" it is not an invitation to be seduced.

v) *Enjoy your own company* and become an interesting person in your own right. Then you really will have something to offer others. Make a list of activities you enjoy doing on your own and pursue them.

w) *Don't sit around waiting to be asked out.* If you're not dating, plan some fun with friends. Don't be dependent on the opposite sex for having fun on weekends. Join a club or a team or a youth group so that you can have fun with others on a regular basis.

Low Cost Activities

- *Rent home videos* and have snacks after. If there is no video shop in your area, start a Video Club and have everyone chip in to buy videos. Perhaps a church youth group could keep a library. Watching a movie doesn't help develop relationships but the snacking afterwards and discussing the values expressed in the movie does.

- *Board games.* Have two or three different games going on at once with fun prizes for the winners.

- *Support your local sports team.* Commit the group to go to all the home games and perhaps some of the games that are on the road for one season.

- *Hiking the local trails.* Check the trail guides for the level of difficulty and for the average length of time needed to cover the route. Plan a picnic on the trail.

- *Beach party.* Bring the volleyball net, frisbee and ghetto blaster. A pool party works too.

- *Ice Skating* party with hot foods afterwards.

- *Music.* The type of music a person listens to most often helps you to figure out what is really their sense of life.

- *Art.* One of the best signs of compatibility is common likes and dislikes in the field of art. Art reveals a sense of life as no other activity can so quickly. A person's sense of life is of great importance in determining how that individual will make value choices.

- Participating in local theater or play.

- Social causes or volunteer work.

- Plan a demonstration or march around some issue relevant to your group. Call the press to observe and then have a party afterwards.

- Creative Arts.
- Throw a party: Birthdays
                   Graduation
                   Someone gets a job
                   Someone changes jobs
                   Moving
                   Meeting new neighbors
                   School is out
                   Back to school
                   First Car
                   Win at sports
                   Any reason will do!

Higher Cost Activities
- Group roller skating or roller blading.
- Group weekend camping or canoe trips.
- Group Skiing...downhill or cross country.
- Winter hayride.
- Horseback riding.
- Travel to a concert, car/boat/computer shows.
- Cooking a special meal for special friends.
- Build a float for school or town or local charity. Come up with an idea and get someone to financially sponsor you. Large locally owned companies are a good place to start, or raise money for your local school or church.
- Retreat weekends offered by church youth groups are an excellent way to get to know others. These retreats are usually developed around a special theme that interests teens. Check out what your local churches offer youth.

Friendly Activities for Two People to Do
Groups are a great way to have lots of fun without making a commitment to any one person. Usually individuals

will be attracted to some in the group more than to others.
One does not want to rush things and spoil a good friendship so on the next list are activities for two people to do
together as friends while they get to know each more
intimately *but* only as friends!

- Invite the person out or over to celebrate their birthday
  with an unusual dinner. A card or funny present would
  be appropriate but nothing mushy or serious yet.

- Any of the sports activities that you both have in
  common.

- Any other activities that perhaps no one else in your
  group is interested in could be a nice way of spending
  time with one person without romance.

- Going to activities together on the transit system or
  a driver picks up passenger(s).

- Asking person to go shopping with you to help select
  a present for someone else or even when buying clothes
  for yourself.

- The important thing to remember when going out alone
  with someone is to have a purpose to the date. That way,
  even if the company turns out to be a disappointment,
  the activity can keep you occupied. When boredom sets
  in, it's not too long before someone is going to make
  a physical move on the other person.

Chapter 7

The Love Test

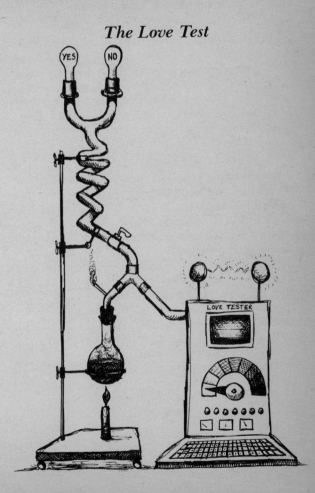

> *"Love is not how you feel.*
> *Love is how you treat a person".*

According to Yale Professor of Psychology Robert Sternberg, PhD, love consists of three essential ingredients — intimacy, passion and commitment — each of which comes more or less to prominence in certain predictable stages. At first passion is usually at its highest, commitment at its lowest, and the foundations for intimacy are beginning to be laid.

Love is What Love Does

The love of which I speak is slow to lose patience.
It always looks for a way to be constructive.
Love is not possessive.
Neither is it anxious to impress,
nor does it cherish inflated ideas on its own importance.
Love has good manners,
and does not pursue selfish advantage.
Love is not touchy or fragile.
It does not keep an account of evil,
or gloat over the wickedness of other people.
On the other hand Love is glad
with all good people whenever truth prevails.
Love does not give up on others.
Love knows no end to its trust, no fading of its hope.
Love outlasts everything.
Love is in fact the one thing
that will be standing when all else has fallen.
Paraphrase of I Corin. 13:4-8

Many people think that it is OK to have sex if they love one another. So sex in North America has become a celebration of love. But what is love? I love Pralines ice cream. That has absolutely nothing to do with sex or marriage. We use the word love so casually for almost anything these days. The problem in the English language is that we have only one word to describe deep feelings for liking the objects, animals, people or activities that we do. I love bright colours...I love horses...I love my family...and I love backpacking in the Rockies! Do you understand what I mean?

The Greeks said "Emotion must warm reason but reason must rule emotion". In real love, your reason is on the throne, ruling your emotions. Gilbert V. Hamilton found that only 15% of love affairs lead to marriage. The American sociologist William Kemphert states that the average person will experience romantic love about 8 times before they marry. That is potentially a lot of sexual partners before one finds the right person. It also means a lot of heartbreak before we get to the altar. How much of a heart will one have left to love their spouse? Won't the pain of past romantic failures invade the marriage?

Love also means different things to each sex. A study was done among college students across the USA. One of the questions put to each of the couples was "Do you love your steady?" Both guy and gal said yes. The next question revealed a different concept or meaning to the word love. They were asked "Do you plan on marrying this person that you say you love?" Eighty-five per cent of the gals answered yes, while only 35% of the guys responded that they had any intention of marrying their steady. What a shock to the ladies, to find out that their boyfriend was saying I love you and yet in his heart had no intention of marrying them.

We see this happening all the time at our counselling centres. As soon as the gal becomes pregnant, the guy changes direction in the relationship. He wants out. Seventy-nine per cent of singles coming in pregnant will be making their decisions without the support of the guy.

Suddenly, he no longer declares his love. Where did it go? My boyfriend told me that he loved me all the time until I got pregnant and then it was "I don't love you that much" or "I wish you weren't pregnant". Obviously pregnancy destroys the romantic loving feelings that were previously experienced. Now, with responsibility on the horizon, love has gone because the feelings are gone. There never was any commitment beyond the feelings.

Many individuals say they are in love but it is really infatuation. The relationships that ended because of a pregnancy were not based on love. Maybe one partner was in love but the other was only infatuated. After I got pregnant I found out that my boyfriend was only infatuated with me; he did not love me at all. What a price to pay to determine a man's true feelings. **There is a better way!**

Yes, there is a way to read the heart of a person before you even kiss. This is true. It is not easy but it is certainly possible. First we must understand what love looks like if we are going to give ourselves sexually in the name of love.

Love is an exchange of vulnerabilities between two people. It is not only loving them at their best but being able to love them at their worst. That is scary.

We need to understand that commitment and concern are much more important components of love than feelings. Love is not just a feeling. It is a decision, a judgment, a promise.

That is why sex gets in the way of knowing if you really love someone. Sexual intimacy feels good. It connects two people together as if the decision and promise have already been made. The problem is that the sexual act has no solid foundation.

To understand the heart and soul of a person one must uncover the outer layers of physical and emotional attraction; one must penetrate the masks. Some people have layer after layer of phoniness and only time will reveal the true character and personality of the individual.

How to Start The Love Test

Step One:

The number one criterion for measuring love is to *stop being sexually active for one year*. If you really want to understand genuine love, you must put the feelings part on the shelf for awhile. You already know they are OK. What you don't know is if there is really the potential for a solid long-term relationship.

It takes one year for a couple to go through the four seasons of change that occur both in nature and in our personalities. You need to be clear headed to evaluate the relationship. This means stopping *all foreplay* as well. Only allow hugging, holding hands and affectionate kissing. Otherwise you have simply created a sexual detour; the physical attractions and feelings are not put on the shelf but are merely re-directed and you are lying to yourself if you think the test will show you anything. You have already failed the *Love Test* because love *can* wait.

There is absolutely no sense continuing the Love Test if step one is not followed.

Many relationships break up at Step One. It is the most difficult part of the test for those who have been sexually active for a long time but it is definitely worth the effort.

Step Two:

With sex out of the picture, it will be easier to see how each person responds in the various areas that build strong, healthy and lasting relationships. During the next year, it will be important to talk to each other about the following areas, and watch and observe how either partner responds in each of these tests.

The Time Test: It is important to go through all the seasons together to discover the many facets of each other's personality; to know their interests and values, to realize their strengths and weaknesses and to see how he/she deals with all kinds of life situations. If the couple is still in their teens, it is especially important to take lots of time. Each person is just starting to blossom into the type of person they will be as adults. There are many changes and experimentations done during the teen years that seldom will be duplicated. When a person is in their twenties or older, 1 to 2 years is plenty of time to know if there is the potential for marriage.

The Chemistry Test: Your whole being responds to the presence of the other. A strong sexual attraction is evident. Without this attraction, the relationship will seldom go beyond friendship or if this attraction is not mutually felt, one of the partners can be hurt deeply. The chemistry test is the easiest test to pass and the hardest, because you can't make it happen. One day you discover you're captivated by the way the person walks, talks, smiles, listens — even the way he/she smells. Everything is right on the outside. If you already have been sexually active, there is a strong likelihood that you both have passed this test with flying colours. No need to rewrite!

The Communication Test: You can talk easily with the other person about anything! You both share your thoughts and feelings openly. You work through your disagreements and conflicts. You really listen to one another and try to understand each other's point of view. You are able to agree or disagree and respect the other person's opinions.

The Friendship Test: You are really good friends. The number one ingredient of successful marriages is being your spouse's best friend. You like to spend time together doing many different kinds of activities. You're comfortable with each other, and like being with each other's friends and families. A strong indication of future problems is when one partner does not like any of the other partner's friends. You know the saying that "birds of a feather flock together". If he/she does not like your friends, does he/she really like you? When there is no sexual activity, the strength of the friendship becomes very clear.

The Real World Test: You are free to love one another. There are no former vows or commitments. You are both free from psychological impediments, from addictions or Sexually Transmitted Diseases, including AIDS. You are realistic about the special problems connected with any differences in age, race, family, religion, and/or background. Note the signs of a dysfunctional relationship listed in chapter 12 under questions.

The Tomorrow Test: You are each confident that the other will be there for you tomorrow and every day after that. You are patient with each other's efforts to learn to love well. You're starting to realize that the beautiful secrets of sexual intimacy can be discovered only in a setting that provides permanence and continuity.

The Commitment Test: You are both willing to pledge your commitment to one another publicly in the presence of witnesses once you are sure of your love for each other. This commitment is marriage and not the common law kind but a signed legal contract or covenant where you both promise to be true to each other.

The Approval Test: The people who know you best, your parents and your friends, approve of your relationship. They can see that he/she brings out the best in you. They feel that you have become a better person. If both parents don't approve, find out why. Parents care and want only what is best for you. Their years of experience and their own past mistakes may help you to avoid a painful marriage.

The Respect Test: You are considerate and courteous in dealing with each other. You respect each other's friends, family, ideas, morals, and religious convictions. You don't use manipulation or blackmail to get your own way. Respect is a very important ingredient in healthy, happy marriages.

The Vision Test: Far from being blind, your love for your partner helps you to see very well just what kind of person he/she is. You know their good points as well as the bad ones, their strengths and their weaknesses. You understand and accept the real person, the one behind the mask. Also vision means you have similar goals and dreams for the future. You have similar ideas about the size of a family and whether you prefer city or country living. Dreams can be different as long as they do not conflict in major areas of married life. If one person wants a large family and the other hates children and never wants to have them, then it's very important to be honest and discuss this big difference.

The Jealousy/Trust Test: You are not possessive of your partner's time or affection. You give each other space to do things and go places without you. You encourage each other to have other friends.

The Values Test: You share common values, morals and priorities on most of the really important things of life. You discuss value questions often. You respect the other's position when it differs from yours, but you also challenge ideas, actions, and attitudes that you can't accept. It is very important to discuss religious values. Different religions pose almost impossible hurdles if both individuals really believe in their particular faith. Love cannot demand change but remember that love cannot continually grow when there is a division between you. Even different denominations within a faith can cause unnecessary damage to the relationship and to one's spiritual life. Be cautious.

The Trust Test: You have complete confidence in your partner. You have learned from experience that you can depend on him/her to be truthful and open to you. You know that he/she will follow through on promises and commitments and support you in time of trouble. That is why couples who have had other partners besides their spouse rarely experience the necessary trust that keeps marriages bonded together.

The Responsibility Test: You are aware of any risks that might be involved in your relationship. You are willing and able to accept full responsibility for the consequences of your actions with one another. You will not expose the other to unnecessary dangers of any kind. Responsibility in school, in sports and in the workplace is evident.

The Prayer Test: You go to church together. You pray frequently for and with each other. You see God in each other and in your love relationship. You seem to be growing closer to God because of your love for one another. This is important because couples who go to church and pray together as a family experience the lowest divorce rate. According to the 1981 US census bureau, only 1 in 1,105 praying marriages ends in divorce!

Step Three:
The Personality Compatibility Test

It is important to realize that people are different. Not just in their looks or sex but different in the very way they process information; different in the way they look at life and solve problems. It is very important to understand your partner. Not to try to change them but to understand why they do what they do. The test is to be taken by each partner. It helps couples to understand their personality traits.

For a copy of the test contact:

Straight Talk
922 Pape Avenue, Suite 200
Toronto, Ontario M4K 3V2
(416) 465-9322

Once the analysis has been completed, mail it to us at the above address and we will return to you a detailed description of your personality as developed by Dr. Leo Roy.

Step Four:
What's important?

In June 1985, *Psychology Today* published the results of a survey. They asked couples married 25 years or more, "What keeps your marriage going?" These are the results in order of importance:

1. **My spouse is my best friend.**
2. I like my spouse as a person.
3. Marriage is a long term commitment.
4. Marriage is sacred.
5. We agree on aims and goals.
6. My spouse has grown more interesting.
7. I want the relationship to succeed.
8. An enduring marriage is important to social stability.
9. We laugh together.
10. I am proud of my spouse's achievements.
11. We agree on a philosophy of life.

12. We agree about our sex life.

13. We agree on how and how often to show affection.

14. I confide in my spouse.

15. We share outside hobbies and interests.

Please discuss these results with your partner. Do you agree on each of these items or are there serious conflicts? If there are, it may be just a matter of time before your differences erupt into serious relationship problems. If the results are similar, you are on the road to establishing a life-long relationship.

Real love includes:

Strong sex interest.

Respect and admiration.

Affection.

Self-giving devotion.

Friendship and fellowship.

The decision to "do the other person good and not evil all the days of one's life".

Checklist to Evaluate Relationship:

Does my partner's vision strengthen my values, my beliefs and my lifestyle?

Does my life vision fit my partner's life vision?

Are we good for each other, motivating each other for good?

Am I comfortable with my partner's expectations of me?

Am I fulfilling my partner's vision?

Does my partner see me as having a legitimate place, other than, "being there" for his/her use?

Do our parents support the relationship and the direction in which it is heading?

Step Five:
We have problems; now what?

Realizing that there are serious problems does not necessarily mean doom and gloom for the future of the relationship.

Many times in our experience with couples going through the love test, one of the partners will end the relationship when he/she sees the truth of their own heart or the truth of their partner's heart. That takes care of the problem. But many times, the couple truly care for each other but past relationships or childhood traumas that are unresolved are causing a breakdown in the present relationship.

It is important that once these problems have been revealed, something is done about them. Usually the hurting person will be counselled at our centre or referred to the proper support group to work through their traumas.

The importance of continuing to abstain sexually is imperative as it allows for total healing of past sexual encounters. If the couple continues to be sexually active, he/she will be unable to recall past sexual traumas because of the present activity. Once all sexual activity stops, it is possible to experience the healing of memories.

Please be aware that relationships are difficult to maintain in the best of times, but when a person carries past hurts, anger and bitterness into the new relationship, it is almost always destined to fail.

If either of the partners in the relationship has experienced the following, please seek professional help or at least support counselling:

Past sexual relationships.

Pornography addiction.

Masturbation addiction.

Sexual abuse.

Physical abuse.

Verbal abuse.

Drug addiction.

Alcohol addiction.

These areas destroy even the best relationships.

Step Six:
Am I really prepared to take the next step?

If everything is getting better in the relationship, and the feelings and commitment to each other are stronger than ever, you may be seriously considering becoming engaged. That's wonderful, but please consider carefully what the main reasons for divorce are and make very sure that you have avoided these major pitfalls. By giving up the sexual activity until marriage, you have the opportunity to experience the true meaning of sex which is a celebration of marriage.

Cosmopolitan magazine conducted a survey during the summer of 1991 and received over 20,000 questionnaires back. The object was to find out the major reasons for divorce. They were as follows:

Lack of emotional intimacy:	81%
Money problems:	65%
Emotional abuse:	63%
Verbal abuse:	59%
Mates distant and remote:	58%
Incompatible goals:	60%
Mate had a drinking problem:	44%
Physical abuse:	29%
Sexual incompatibility:	72%

Listed as follows:

Wife loses passion for husband: 70%

Husband loses passion for wife: 30%

Infidelity became a problem: 66%

Wives verbally abused husbands: 16%

Wives lying regularly to husbands: 12%

Step Seven:
The final frontier.

Now that you have gone through the year together and passed each step with flying colours, you may be ready to set the wedding date. Before you do there is one more point to consider. **There is one more step you can take if you dare!**

And I mean that very seriously. This step is NOT for everyone. But this step is for those who want to be sure of their destiny.

Commit your future marriage partner to God. Let God be the ultimate match-maker. Don't give God your order. Ask God to bring to you the partner of His choice. The Creator of the universe will hear your prayer. It is a dangerous prayer to pray and one not to be taken lightly.

There is not just one person who is compatible with you. Either one of you could meet another person and be very happy in marriage with that individual. There are several individuals in each major city who would and could make you very happy as long as you are the right personality type for each other. That is why match-making or dating services do so well. You can do well without asking God, BUT if you're daring and want to see what God would do for you then TAKE THE PLUNGE LIKE I HAVE!

I have been practicing chastity now for 10 years. I prayed this prayer. God has not shown me who is to be my husband yet but I know it will be His choice for my life. That will be my next book!

Chapter 8

The Greatest Gift of All

The true value of a gift is proportionate to the sacrifice which you made in order to give it.

The first gift I received from my sweetheart was a 22 karat gold necklace with a gold heart pendant. His name was engraved on one side of the heart and my name was on the other. I never took that necklace off, no matter where I went or what I was doing. It was very special to me.

After we broke up, I kept wearing the necklace. It was my only piece of real jewelry. He is married now and he dated other women before he married. What if he gave the identical gold necklace to every woman he fell in love with? Not to every woman he dated or liked, but to the ones with whom he had a special relationship. He falls in love with Sue, buys her a 22 karat gold necklace...she leaves him. Then he meets Nancy and she is awesome. He buys her a 22 karat gold necklace with his and her name engraved on the heart. After two years he leaves her and falls in love with Julie...then Brenda...finally he meets Jennifer and also buys her a 22 karat gold necklace. Things go well...they become engaged...they get married.

After the honeymoon, Jennifer goes shopping in a grocery store and there she meets all the women who are wearing the identical 22 karat gold necklace given to them by her husband. How would she feel about her gift? I would think maybe the guy got a discount! Or bought a dozen at a time. Because the same necklace was given to every other woman he professed to be in love with, the gift has lost its meaning. It is still 22 karat gold but because the meaning is lost, the value and treatment of the gift is totally different.

Some might toss the necklace in a drawer and never wear it again. Others may give it away, sell it or even throw it in the garbage, as one young woman did when she found out her ring had been worn by her boyfriend's former girlfriend!

If there is no obvious sacrifice to give the gift, it will not be treated with care and respect. And so it is with sex.

William Kemphert, a noted American sociologist says that the average North American will fall in love 8 times before marriage and 1 and 1/2 times after marriage. If this is the case, then having sex with a person because one loves them means there will be quite a few sexual partners before marriage, all in the name of love.

For example, I will use my own experience. I am changing the names to protect the innocent. The first man I fall in love with, I go all the way because we love each other. "Bill...Bill...I love you" so I have sex with Bill because I love him. After my abortion, I no longer have the same feelings for Bill so we break up. Then I meet Henry. "Henry...Henry...I love you". Since I've had sex before, it's pretty obvious that as soon as I declare my love to Henry. I'm expected to go all the way. I love Henry, so I have sex with Henry. We later break up. "Ben... Ben...I love you Ben". Therefore I have sex with Ben. Again we break up. "Bart...Bart...I love you Bart". Oh no! He's a Simpson...I have to find someone else!

How will sex be special if I have given myself totally to each of these men I say I love? Was there any sacrifice on my part to bring something special into the marriage? No. I gave myself to every man I said, "I love you" to. It wasn't hard for me to refuse to have sex with someone I didn't like.

It is certainly hard for me today to hold back giving myself to a man that I have strong feelings for. That takes courage, and great amounts of sacrifice. I take great pride in being a secondary virgin. At least I have a gift that has not been given during the last ten years. If I could live my life over again, I would not be sexually active until my wedding night because I realize now the greatest gift I could ever give my husband is my sexual innocence. Ten years of purity is better than none at all!

During one of my presentations, one young teen agreed that sex was very special and made a decision to wait until she was in love. She was not going to just throw her virginity away. She wanted it to mean something. She felt that she would give herself totally to the first person that she would declare her love to.

That sounds very romantic but considering the number of possible times the average person will fall in love what does she intend to give the last person she falls in love with...*the leftovers?*

What special gift was I giving to the man I was engaged to? A heart that had been broken more than once. A body damaged by the abortions I experienced. During the five years I tried to get pregnant, nothing happened. He was not getting the best of me. Yes, in some ways I had learned from the past relationships. I was more mature than when I was a teenager. But that would have happened naturally anyway. Was I really saving the very best person that I could be for the one that I would spend the rest of my life with? I think not. You know the old expression... "Once bitten, twice shy".

I now believe that sex is the one thing in all of life that was not meant to be shared with any one else but the one to whom you are married.

Two virgins who marry create their own private world that no one else has ever entered. Intimate moments never shared with any one else. The inner circle. No ghosts. They create their own language of love. The wonderful thing about sexual intimacy is its power to bond two people together like nothing else on earth.

However, the more sexual partners we have, the less able we are to bond with one person in that unique way.

The wonderful news is that it is never too late to change your behavior. We have seen couples who were sexually active stop completely until marriage. Some couples had even lived together then moved apart and stopped all sexual activity until they were married. Even couples with children have chosen to stop sexual activity until marriage!

Secondary virgins find a wonderful opportunity to develop the other aspects of their friendships and to experience inner healing from past hurts and relationships. They acquire a new understanding of sex as a celebration of marriage. They look forward to the time when they marry and become one.

Couples who stopped being sexually active find that the sexual intimacy they experience in marriage is greater than it had ever been when they were single. What made it more special was their decision to abstain from the sexual activity that had hindered their assurance that their love for each other was real. They knew that they had chosen freely to marry and that there was no guilt because of sexual activity.

Sometimes sex gets in the way of knowing real love. Sex feels good, but that does not necessarily mean that the relationship or the marriage will be good.

Remember that if you have been sexually abused, you still have your gift of chastity. Sexual abuse twists and degrades what should be a beautiful experience freely given in marriage. Please realize that you have never given your gift. You have been violated in a way beyond your comprehension and your ability to "say no". This is not your fault.

If you have been sexually abused, please get help. Counselling can assist you to come to grips with your childhood nightmares. Proper counselling can assist you in healing memories and allow you to deal with the pain in a positive way to allow you the best opportunity to experience healthy relationships, both singly and in marriage.

Couples who have married and have feelings of regret over their sexual history before marriage can also experience a beautiful healing in this area. Husbands and wives ask each other's forgiveness, each declaring that if they could live their lives over, they would chose to wait until marriage and give themselves only to each other.

Then they agree on a period of sexual abstinence. During this time they court each other and set a date, possibly their anniversary, to renew their marriage vows; then they consummate their renewed vows. They no longer need to feel that they are victims of their past and that life is out of control. They have stopped, taken control of their past and created a new future. It is never too late.

Chapter 9

Benefits of Waiting Until Marriage

"That which does not grow, dies".
                                        Leo Buscaglia, PhD

Plan Your Future

By saying no to sex until marriage, you are giving yourself the greatest opportunity to accomplish career goals. There may be other setbacks but they are usually short term in comparison to caring for a family. Over half of teen moms drop out of school. There are many things in life that are accomplished more easily when you are single.

There is plenty of time for marriage. Take the single years and find out who you really are. Pursue your talents and follow your dreams. Develop beautiful friendships with the same sex and with the opposite sex. Many a career goal has had to be changed, some indefinitely, because of sexual activity or because of the consequences of that activity. You have one life to live. There is no dress rehearsal.

Freedom From Disease

Two virgins who marry do not get sexually transmitted diseases. There will be no fear of this happening. If one of the partners has had previous sexual partners there is the possibility of disease. Remember the AIDS awareness commercial: when you have sex with someone, you are sleeping with all the partners that one has had before. Don't throw yourself away on casual, short term relationships. Save yourself for that special one.

More and more research is being done connecting lifestyle with disease. The human body was not designed for multiple sexual partners. Teenage girls who become sexually active also have a higher risk of cancer of the cervix if they have more than one sexual partner in their teen years.

Trust/Respect

Someone who has the strength to wait until marriage before being sexually active, especially by not giving in to the person they love, will gain the trust and respect of their partner. It shows that he/she can be trusted to be left alone with the opposite sex without giving in to sexual temptation. Fidelity and faithfulness are believable when a person has waited. It is very hard to believe that your partner would not give in sexually, under the right circumstances, if they gave in to others before you. Trust and respect in a marriage are important foundations to building a strong family.

Help Others

Energy is sometimes defined as the "capacity to do work". In his book *Human Sexual Ecology,* Robert E. Joyce says that "sexual energy may be understood as the capacity to share. Sharing is the particular kind of work that is proper to sexual energy".

Teens who are not sexually active and who avoid substance abuse and heavy dating have boundless energy. They are not thinking about the next party, or day dreaming about the love of their life. We all have a great deal of energy but when we misuse it, we have little left for anything else. That is why many times, studying gets boring and marks go down. Little time is spent with family and social gatherings because of the interest in sex, drugs or alcohol.

Energy that is not used up negatively is there for helping other people. I know many teens who are far more active in social concerns than adults. These teens feel good about themselves and are developing strong character.

Develop Friendships Without Sexual Overtones

Many young people are growing up these days without a brother or a sister. Where do they learn to relate to or even understand how the male or female mind works? Even in families with a father, he is often absent. There are 168 hours in each week. Who is getting all this time?

Families should be a safe environment to learn and to understand all of the emotions we possess without sexual overtones. We need many years of interaction before we enter into a sexually intimate relationship. Along with family dynamics, we need to develop friends outside of the home, both male and female. As human beings we are learning how to interact with each other and how to handle all of our human emotions — attraction, anger, love, laughter, sadness, etc. without sexual overtones or sexual expression.

Obviously there are many elements that create healthy, successful relationships but we are only dealing with the sexual area in this book. It certainly makes life easier when one can work through their emotions without sexual pressures. There is far less damage done to another individual if there are no sexual ties.

My only brother is 13 years younger than I am and my father, although he cared for us materially, came from the old school that said you never show your feelings to your children. I never felt loved by my dad. I know now that he loved me but I did not perceive that love while I was growing up. I hardly knew my dad. Where was I to learn how men think and behave when I had little to no contact with males in a safe nurturing environment?

I believe that I became sexually active because I was looking for Daddy's love just like Dr. Appleton says in his book "Fathers and Daughters". He uses the word obsessed. He says that teens who don't receive proper love from their father become obsessed with boys to help establish their identity and their femininity.

Now that I am not sexually active, I have wonderful relationships with guys who are like brothers to me. It has helped me to understand men more clearly. My brother is a grown man now and we also have a good relationship. We play and tease each other and have great fun with no fear whatsoever. Actually, I have noticed that even with male friends I can never be that carefree and trusting because they are not blood related. So do be careful.

I find that when I am really down and sad, I call my female friends first so I can let my hair down totally and not worry about the future. I have heard many a sad tale of opposite sex friends who when one of the individuals was down, was comforted by the other, but the sexual attraction became overwhelming. There were many regrets; they never wanted the relationship to develop sexually. It has ruined many a friendship, so be careful.

These opposite sex friendships have helped me feel good about myself as a person. I know I am liked for the person I am on the inside. I feel like a blanket of love envelopes me everywhere I go. It is a wonderful feeling. When I was sexually active, I only had the loving feeling while being held by my man. Two, three hours a week may be, some times more, but that was it. Now I feel connected and loved all the time. It's different, but it is so comforting. I prefer the world I'm in now compared to the extreme loneliness I experienced before.

Sense of Wonder

Ask any one if they remember the 99th time they had sex. They will be lucky if they can remember who it was with let alone any other details. How about the 19th time? Or the 12th time? But ask any one if they remember the very first time they went all the way. It is an instant replay. For most females, the first time seems to have been more negative but for males, the first time seems to have been very positive.

The experience of couples who were virgins until their wedding night, also seems to be positive. Obviously without experience, it may be a bit awkward, but because of their deep love and trust in each other they grow together in their experience.

How sad for the person who looks back to their first sexual experience and it is with other than their spouse. What better plan than to bring the first time to the wedding night or the honeymoon after the vows have been taken. No guilt. No comparisons either. Intimacy means an experience shared by only 2 people. You are able to create your own language of love. You enter your own private world together that no other person has ever entered.

Now, as a secondary virgin, I believe that I will benefit from the change in my lifestyle. I have invested 10 years in my future marriage. It is so exciting to know that it is never too late to change!

Learn Discipline and Self Control

Learning to control one's sexual desires may help us in other areas of life as well. This kind of discipline helps us learn to control anger and other powerful emotions that can be used either for good or for harm. We learn to love with our hearts and minds first and only after marriage with our bodies. Can you imagine that you could love someone so much that you could marry that person without ever having more than some beautiful moments of kissing? You both have shared so many other experiences together.

You can just walk and not talk yet you feel so comfortable together. You can laugh together. You can play together. You can work together. You have developed a language all your own. When your loved one cries, you feel such pain and share intimately in the grief. You want to take the pain away. Your love is pure because there is nothing sexual to overpower your head and heart. There is progressive trust and respect for each other. You want the very best for each other.

Practising self control before marriage will make it much easier to practise self control during those times in one's life when it becomes impossible to express love sexually, ie: hospitalization, recovery from illness or injury, periods of separation or permanent disability. It's a good feeling knowing that your spouse is faithful no matter what the circumstance.

Marry for the Right Reasons

Without sexual expressions, two people have the greatest opportunity to make their decision for marriage with their heads and their hearts. They are not being pressured into marriage because they have been sexually active for some time now or because the woman is pregnant. They both see their lives together. Almost like a soul mate.

Make sure not to rush into marriage. I have counselled situations in which the couple were virgins but they married less than six months after meeting each other. They rushed into marriage because they felt they could not abstain sexually any longer than that.

Happy Sex Life

Two virgins or two secondary virgins have the potential to experience the best possible sex between two human beings. The main reason is they choose to wait until marriage because they understand that sex is a celebration of marriage.

A counsellor wrote Ann Landers saying that in her twenty years of marriage counselling, she had heard the same thing over and over again. Couples would say their sex life was great when they were single, but once they got married it went to hell!

I produced a video called "Chastity: A Question of Choice" and went across Canada interviewing couples who were virgins or secondary virgins when they got married. They say their sex life is a little bit of heaven on earth. Quite a difference between the quotes, don't you think?

One elderly lady came up to me after one of my presentations and encouraged me to keep saying what I'm saying. She said she and her husband were both virgins when they married and they taught each other everything they know. She seemed so proud of that. She also mentioned that sex gets better with age, like a good wine. Sex is spiritual, not just physical. So when you add years of sharing all of life's ups and downs together in sexual union, it's got to be great. She did mention that after raising 5 children and being in their late sixties, they had slowed down compared to years ago. Well, looking at this silver haired lady, I could understand that and nodded. I was not ready for her answer. She said, "Yes, we are only twice a week now".

I tell you, when I see those olden goldies and they are smiling, I know what's going on!

Freedom to See Children as They Really are — Special!

I experienced my first pregnancy as a teen. I was single, scared and confused. My boyfriend threatened to leave me unless I had an abortion. I certainly did not see a child as a wonderful gift enhancing our relationship. I saw it as my worst nightmare!

A girl in a crisis pregnancy misses out on the opportunity to experience the wonder and miracle that is growing inside of her even though it was conceived from an act of love. It is not their love child. In crisis, almost 100,000 women abort their babies each year in Canada alone. In the US, it is over one and a half million per year and worldwide over 65 million abortions annually. Obviously, these pregnancies do not bring happiness.

Ideally, the knowledge of a forthcoming child should be exciting news, bonding the parents together as they realize what their love has created!

Greatest Chance for Successful Marriage

Statistics Canada says that over 40% of marriages end in divorce. Over 10% are legally separated and over 20% of marriages are unhappy. Yet couples who wait until marriage before being sexually active have an extremely low divorce rate.[1]

According to the 1981 US Census, if a couple married in a church and continued to go to church, the divorce rate was 2%. But if they also prayed together as a family as well as attending church, the divorce rate was 1 in 1,105 marriages; less than .009% divorce rate. You have heard the old saying "a family that prays together stays together". I guess it really is true.

Choosing to wait certainly makes sense if one wants to experience the greatest chance for a happy successful marriage. Broken homes and broken hearts abound in North America because we throw away our teen years carelessly and casually. It doesn't have to be that way.

Chapter 10

Secondary Virginity

The *People* magazine cover story for April 20, 1992 read, "In a $30,000 gown and with her 20-year-old son at her side, the TV star (Connie Sellecca of P.S.I. Luv U) weds the ET host (John Tesh of Entertainment Tonight) after a year of romance — but no sex. This, Tesh says with a grin, 'is going to be *some* honeymoon!'"

I am so thankful for this new designation given to men and women who have decided to change the direction of their lives and make a new start. Like me, they have decided to stop being sexually active until marriage. Even if they have been married before and had children like the TV stars John Tesh and Connie Sellecca, it doesn't matter. That is what secondary virginity is all about.

There are three facets to virginity: physical, emotional and spiritual. I have lost forever my physical virginity, but have regained and strengthened my emotional and spiritual virginity. It's truly as if I'd never lost it. I am more of a virgin than a virgin who has experienced everything but vaginal penetration. Yes, they are physically virgins, which I'm not, and they avoid all the physical consequences of intercourse but they may experience as many marital problems as anyone else!

Chastity is purity of mind, body and soul. One must protect all three aspects of virginity. Virgins who have experienced everything but vaginal intercourse can, of course, stop doing that and regain their emotional and spiritual purity; but if they don't, when they say they have waited until marriage they are really deceiving themselves.

The decision is not an easy one nor should a person expect to be 100% successful as soon as the decision is made. A lot will depend on determination and knowledge. If one does not know how to change, then it may work for awhile, and then boom, you're at it again. It's like cigarette smoking. Some people quit cold turkey and never take a puff again. Most people find that they quit many times before they're successful.

Don't be disappointed. Remember that if you want to play a musical instrument, you won't play it perfectly the first time around. What if I said to you "hit one wrong note and I cut off your fingers!" You would never try to play, would you? We all know that before you can be good at something, you usually have to experience failure. And so it is with secondary virginity. Your goal is to be chaste until marriage. Realize that failure is possible.

What we're saying is *"Congratulations"*. You have made a great decision. Keep concentrating on your goal: no sex until marriage. If you fail, analyze your mistakes. Ask yourself, "What was different tonight from other nights. What are my weak points? What can I do to avoid this situation again?" Learn from your mistakes. Pick yourself up and try again.

If you find that you and your boyfriend/girlfriend can't seem to keep your hands to yourselves, a three month breakup may be necessary to regain control of the passions. Maintain the relationship by phone and by letter. Write poetry to each other. Be creative. Find ways to express your devotion without seeing each other. Many couples have found that the three month separation really helps to bring their passions under control.

It is important to set new guidelines in what is acceptable in the area of kissing. Once a person has been sexually active, it is very difficult to stay calm and cool as the body has a history of responding under foreplay. Many couples also decide not even to kiss passionately or French kiss until marriage. They found that this was the point of decision making. Holding hands, hugging and affectionate kissing did not cause arousal problems but French kissing did.

I have decided also that only affectionate kissing will be acceptable until marriage. I expect my man to respect my decision and hopefully, he will have come to that decision himself before we ever date romantically. It makes life a lot easier when both partners have the same point of view.

Remember that if you have been sexually abused, you have *never* given your gift. You were exploited and victimized by someone much older than you who knew better. It is not your fault. As a little child, you were totally innocent even if you were running around naked in front of an adult. You didn't know any better. *The adult did!*

It doesn't matter if your body enjoyed it or if you did. It doesn't matter if you have become sexually active with adults now as a result of the sexual abuse as a child. *You still have not given your gift.* Stop now! You still have a chance. Get counselling for sexual abuse. It is important to receive inner healing so that you can appreciate the beauty that the sex act was meant to be. Sex is a celebration of marriage. That is not what you experienced. Take control of your life now. By stopping sexual activity and receiving counselling, you too can look forward to your wedding night. You have a gift that you have taken control of and you can freely choose to give your gift to whomever you want.

I feel good about myself now. I have a gift to give to the man I marry. I am a secondary virgin and am proud that I've invested ten years into this lifestyle. I believe that the man I marry will appreciate and respect my choice to save myself for him. It would have been better if I had never become sexually active but I have stopped instead of continuing on in that lifestyle and that is a triumph!

Chapter 11

What Do I Do With My Broken Heart?

"Fear of grief is not an irrational fear. Grief is real and our normal response to loss. We risk it each time we allow ourselves to love someone. Appropriate grieving is different than endless mourning. It includes healing, too".

Barbara Cook

In almost every other area except relationships, we give ourselves a chance to heal before we get involved again. When they suffer a broken heart, most people find a person as soon as possible to fall in love with to replace the emptiness experienced by the loss. That is the *worst* thing a person can do.

If you broke your leg, you would get medical attention. You might be hospitalized for awhile and your leg would certainly be in a cast. When the cast was removed, you would start slowly exercising your leg. You would not get right back into skiing as soon as the cast was removed. The leg would not be able to handle the stress.

Well, what about a broken heart? It needs time to rest and then slowly work back into a relationship. It's OK to grieve after a broken relationship. It's OK to cry or not be interested in spending time with friends. It's OK for a season to allow yourself to heal. *You need time.*

Just like time is necessary to heal the broken leg so time is necessary to heal a broken heart. You owe it to yourself to take care of the only heart you have. If you heal properly, you will find that you are not taking problems from the past relationship into the future one. There will be enough time between the two relationships. It truly will be a new beginning.

The following outline is what the grieving process is all about. Understanding what's happening can help you be a better and stronger person than before.

Remember that these stages may not happen exactly in this order but are fairly close. The stages of grieving are normal for family breakups as well as death. A broken heart hurts in the same way as death. A broken heart hurts in the same way and sometimes feels worse, especially if the relationship has lasted a long time and marriage was a strong possibility.

Shock & Denial:

If you were totally unprepared for the breakup, this is very natural. You can hardly believe that this is really happening to you. You feel totally out of control. The carpet has just been pulled out from under you. You may feel almost dizzy and disorientated. Almost numb. This is very normal.

During this time, there will be little interest in activities, relationships and life in general. Everything seems a waste. This is a very natural way to feel. Allow yourself to slow down for awhile. Remember, I said for awhile. A healthy time frame is 4-6 weeks of little or no activity. If you go beyond this time period, be careful because it can become pathological.

Expressiveness:

After the initial shock has worn off many people become either life of the party types or introverted and withdraw from entering new relationships. Perhaps only trusted friends will be contacted. That is OK. Over-expressiveness is a reaction to the hurt and that will balance itself out in time. Don't worry about it unless you are hurting people or getting hurt yourself. Don't push for another relationship prematurely.

Bargaining & Rationalizing:

We say we are better off without them anyway. The person was dragging us down. We try and tear apart the relationship and devalue it so we don't feel the loss as much. We say things like, "Well, if I had lost 30 lbs., he never would have left" or, "If I had bought that Corvette instead of the Chevy, she wouldn't have left me for so and so!" "If I hadn't gone away to college, she wouldn't have found another man". Or we try to rationalize that we are better off without the other person. Either way, we are not being honest with ourselves.

Anger:

During this anger stage, we start blaming others for causing the breakup. We may become very angry at our family or our friends if we feel they did not support the relationship as much as we think they should have. We may be very angry now at the person who broke our heart. First we wanted him/her back no matter what. Now, we hate their guts. We feel betrayed and lied to. We feel deceived since their declarations of love were not eternal as he/she promised.

Guilt/Depression:

This is the lowest point in the process. It is the most painful but it is also a sign that hope and healing are just around the corner. All the sudden, we blame ourselves for the breakup. We feel guilty. We look back over the relationship and see all the mistakes we made. We might even see the warning signs of trouble in the relationship. That's when the worst sort of depression sets in. You almost feel like giving up. You may not feel like going on in life. I know I have felt that way many times.

Note: It takes at least one year to go through all the stages of grieving. One must experience each season without their loved one. Each birthday and holiday must be experienced without that person. If the relationship lasted less than a year, then it may not take a full year.

But if you have gone through all the seasons with each other, then one must grieve each of those moments together. After my fiancé and I broke up, (we had lived together for 5 years) I grieved strongly for the first two years. I never even dated anyone for almost 5 years. It was a very traumatic separation that took us both totally by surprise.

Acceptance:

This is the first sign of deep healing. We do not rationalize or run away from our feelings. We accept what has happened to us. It is over. The memories both good and bad will always be a part of us. We will never be the same again. It doesn't mean that we can't be a better person, we certainly can be, but we are different. We are the sum total of our past experiences. I am what I am today because of what I have gone through. I don't cry over my past anymore but look forward with anticipation to my future. I am stronger for the pain that I have endured. I am more sensitive to other people's feelings and hurts. I understand the value of honesty and respect in relationships more than ever before.

Recovery:

Once acceptance is felt, you are ready to move forward in life. There may be new decisions to make. Perhaps you moved to the town of your loved one. Now there is no need to stay in this town anymore. Perhaps you will move on. I left the Kitchener-Waterloo area after my breakup and moved to Toronto. I made an entire break with my past. For me that was the best thing to do. You are not running away but are seeking new opportunities elsewhere. Start something that you have always wanted to do but never before had the time or support. Take a holiday, one that you have always wanted to take.

After my father died there was a time of inactivity and hesitancy. Now I see the family, especially my mom, have accepted life without him and she has made changes to accommodate her singleness. She has opened a little grocery store. She did some renovations in the house to suit the new shape of our family. That is part of accepting the loss of the departed one and looking forward to the future.

Forgiveness:

If there is any bitterness towards the person who broke your heart, it is very important to forgive that person. It doesn't matter whether you are a religious person or not. The bitterness and unforgiveness will only destroy you and any future chance of having a successful relationship. Unforgiveness keeps you tied to the person in your past. Your new love will do or say something that relates to the old love or reminds you of the hurt and you might lash out at your present love. You are reacting to your past. Forgiveness sets you free to love again. Forgiveness allows you to love with a reconstructed heart, a healed heart not a piece of a heart or a broken one. You owe it to yourself to forgive.

Reconciliation of Broken Relationships:

This reconciliation refers to relationships other than with your steady. Perhaps you broke off relationships with family or some friends because of your hurt. Family and friends are too important to leave them with open wounds. Just a little apology to the individual could mean a world of difference in the future.

Hope:

Once a full year has passed, you can take a deep breath and be open to developing new friendships. Perhaps the love of your life is waiting for you just around the corner. You are not on the rebound. You are not out for revenge, to hurt others as you have been hurt. You are simply ready to give and receive love.

I am ready. Actually I think I have been ready for several years now but I'm not interested in romance for the sake of marriage. I want friendships more than anything. I believe that from a beautiful friendship will develop a beautiful courtship leading to marriage.

Chapter 12

Questions Most Asked by Teens

You Look Like A Dream!...so, go back to sleep!

Who holds the world record for the longest sexual encounter?

The Sea Turtle. Fifty-two hours each time. Now you know why they move so slowly!

Why does so much sex go on around drugs or alcohol?

That is a good question. Many people have said that they don't know what came over them. Perhaps they have been friends for years and have never been sexually intimate with each other. But under the influence of drugs or alcohol, a person's judgment becomes impaired. All the sudden a person tosses his or her values to the wind, for the pleasures of the moment.

Does sex hurt the first time?

A woman may have pain the first time she has intercourse. For women, the problem is the setting. It may be less than perfect and the relationship is not within a commitment. Fear keeps the vaginal muscles tense which causes pain. Studies show that married women have greater enjoyment of the sex act than single women do. *Redbook* also found that religious women are the greatest sexual partners, probably because once they marry they are free to enjoy their spouses without shame.

How come people blame their teen years for most of the STD problems?

I think there are two reasons for that. If young teens starts being sexually active, it is quite likely they will encounter 2-8 partners before reaching their twenties. Once a person is in his or her twenties, relationships usually start lasting longer and lead to marriage.

The second reason is related to the first. Dr. Karen Hein, director of the Adolescent AIDS Program at Montefiore

Hospital in New York City, believes teenaged girls are more vulnerable to HIV than adult women because many of them have yet to form a protective layer of cells that line the vagina. That could also apply to other STDs and perhaps explain why cancer of the cervix increases in women who have multiple partners especially in their teen years.

Why don't they make condoms out of stronger rubber?

Ever since condoms have been on the market, men have complained of the thickness. The thicker the condom, the less sensation a man feels. Some men report that wearing a condom during intercourse is like shaking hands with your gloves on.

**My mother says I can't date until I'm 16.
What do you think?**

Well, I can only tell you what the studies are showing. The McDowell Research Institute found that if a person starts dating at age 12, the chances of being sexually active by age 18 are over 90%. If you wait until 14 before dating, the chances of being sexually active by age 18 are 67%. But if you wait until 16 before dating, then the chances of being sexually active are only 19%. I guess your mother understands this. Think about it another way. One cannot get a drivers licence in most provinces or states until age 16. Even though a person might physically be able to drive a car when they are much younger, the law states that one must be 16 years old, then write a beginners exam, then get a beginners licence before learning to drive. Sixteen years of age seems to be a good average age of maturity. That is what is missing earlier: maturity. Perhaps your mother thinks the same way about dating. Don't worry, you are going to live an average of 78 years if you're a woman and 72 if you're a man. Accept what you can't change and have fun with what you are allowed to do. It's just a matter of time until you're old enough to date.

How do you know if you are really in love? Can you tell if the person is only interested in a sexual relationship?

Because love is a word that can mean many different things, it is very important to know what kind of love the person is implying. It could be "I love being with you…"I love you at this time in my life"…"I love your body" or "I love what people say about me because I'm going out with you". Do you get the picture? I've had many guys say they loved me but that did not mean they wanted to marry me! Please read Chapter 7 which is the *Love Test*. That will help. The other question you asked was if you can tell if the person is only interested in sex. *There is only one way of knowing if the relationship is based on love not sex and that is you must stop being sexually active or don't start.* There must be a lengthy period of abstinence to determine the degree of love.

I have counselled many a couple in my office where the guy or girl had been declaring their eternal love to the other, only now to be saying, "I really thought I loved you, but this pregnancy shows me now that I don't love you as much as I thought I did". Please don't risk your heart in finding out the hard way. Remember love is free. If you have to give something to get love it is not love.

Why is artificial birth control promoted so much if there can be so many problems with it?

The real reason is money. Birth control is a major industry in North America. Figure it out. There are over 50 million women on the birth control pill. Multiply that by the cost per package. Condom sales have risen over 300% in the last 3 years. Natural Family Planning is free. No one makes money from NFP.

I'm only 13 years old and not really interested in girls right now but I think I'd like to be married someday. My friends say I'm gay. What do you think?

You are perfectly normal. Perhaps your 13 year old friends who are chasing the girls are starting too early. It is typical for guys in their early teens not to be interested in girls. This will change. Usually by the time you are 16, things are looking different. That doesn't mean you have to be chasing girls. Many guys who plan on going to college or university don't date seriously. They really don't want to get involved before they finish their education, or they are really into sports or have other talents.

I can't seem to say no to guys who make passes at me. Why am I like this?

This usually stems from one of the following:

- Poor father and daughter relationship during puberty.

- Father tries to keep you from growing up.

- Sexual abuse during childhood which automatically prepares the body to participate sexually because of the past conditioning. As soon as a young man puts his arm around you, your mind shuts down and your body goes along with whatever the guy wants. He thinks you are easy but really your mind has left the scene — only the body stays behind.

- Starved for affection and willing to get it any way you can.

- Weakened under the influence of drugs or alcohol.

- Suicidal tendencies.

- Low self-esteem

Please get help in this area. It is very difficult to try and change on your own. Call any of our Straight Talk Offices or the Youth Hot Line for the centre nearest you.

Isn't the pill still the best method of birth control?

The World Health Organization states that Natural Family Planning is the most effective way of planning your family. The effective rate for married couples is 98.5%. Only sterilization has a higher effective rate. "Fit for Life II: Living Health" by Harvey and Marilyn Diamond also recommends Natural Family Planning. Chapter 2 and Appendix I have more information about Natural Family Planning. It is so accurate that a couple can learn about their bodies to the degree that they can use the method to avoid a pregnancy or to achieve a pregnancy! It is not the old 'rhythm method'. That method is the horse and buggy of Natural Family Planning. Check your 'Yellow Pages' for the office nearest you. Catholic churches often have teacher couples who can train married couples in this method.

How do I get a guy to notice me?

The first thing to realize is that not every guy that you like will like you back the same way and vice versa. That's life. Accept it. If the guy is not involved naturally in any part of your world, you are asking for trouble. It means one or the other has to leave their friends, etc. to spend time with the other person. So perhaps for the time being, it would be better to concentrate on your circle of friends. If, however, the guy is in your circle of friends, in the same class or has similar hobbies or interests, it will be a lot easier. Remember that best friends have the most successful marriages. Because he crosses into your world regularly, friendship should happen quite naturally because you both have things in common. If the guy does not pick up on your interest then perhaps he is just not interested or not ready for anything more. Take it slowly. You cannot make a rose bloom before its time. It is the same with friendships and romance. So enjoy yourself and watch the relationship grow. See chapter 6 on creative dating which may give you ideas how to get closer to this person casually without over exposing your heart.

How can I tell if I'm in an abusive relationship?

He/She

- Won't let you talk to other opposite sex friends and is very jealous.

- Continually criticizes what you wear and what you do.

- Likes to scare you by driving fast or doing reckless things.

- Wants to know where you are and who you are with at all times.

- Tells other people about things you did or said that embarrass you or make you feel stupid.

- Gets "carried away" during horseplay and hurts you, or holds you down and makes you feel helpless until you give in or feel humiliated.

- Becomes very angry about trivial things — like not being ready on time for a date or wearing the "wrong" clothes.

- Criticizes your friends and asks you to stop seeing them.

- Is often depressed or withdrawn but won't talk about feelings.

- Comes from an abusive home.

- Becomes angry or violent when using alcohol or drugs.

- Forces you to do anything sexually that you don't feel ready to do — either by physical force or by put-downs, threats to leave or other emotional pressures.

- Continually tells you you're stupid, lazy, fat, ugly, and so on.
- Makes degrading jokes about men/women or displays interest in other men/women to make you scared or upset.
- Makes threats about hitting you, hurting your friends or pets, or suicide if you don't obey. Or if they have *ever* hit you, no matter how sorry they were afterwards!

How can you be a secondary virgin if you've already had sex?

Secondary virginity is a term coined in the eighties to indicate a renewed lifestyle. You are right, one cannot go back and become a physical virgin but sex is very emotional and spiritual as well as physical. The physical is lost forever but the emotional and the spiritual can be retrieved just as if it never happened. It gives a fresh start for those of us who blew it the first time around. I am practicing chastity as a way of life. I will benefit emotionally and spiritually by making this dramatic change in my life. Those who are virgins and wait until marriage have it all. They have kept the physical, emotional and the spiritual part of them for one person. I lost the physical but I have pure emotions and spirit to give my husband in marriage. Those who continue to have sex before marriage, and then in marriage have lost physically, emotionally and spiritually in this area unless a time of reflection and healing comes after the marriage.

It's very important to remember is that being a virgin doesn't mean going almost all the way. In other words, everything but vaginal penetration has been experienced by the couple. The girl technically is a virgin only in the physical sense, but she is not really a virgin in the emotional or spiritual sense because she has bonded to the other person and has full knowledge. She only deceives herself if she thinks she has really saved herself for her husband. Of course there are less physical consequences if she is still a virgin. A secondary virgin has more going for her than a virgin who gives 99% of herself and thinks she is doing something really honorable. She lacks the emotional and spiritual purity which a secondary virgin has. Don't get involved in going part way sexually.

My parents don't like my boyfriend. What do I do?

That is a good question. In this day and age, many don't respect their parents wishes but it sounds like you do. Remember that your parents love you very much and because of their age have a maturity that you don't have as yet. They can also see things in the relationship that you can't see. A good thing to do is ask them specifically what they don't like about your boyfriend. Write them down and see if your boyfriend is able to work on them and change.

Maybe your boyfriend has dropped out of school. He works for a few months and then he quits and collects unemployment and has fun with his friends during the summer. Then he runs out of money and he gets a job again until the next summer and then he quits again.

Your parents are very concerned because they don't see in him the qualities necessary to provide for a family. They feel you will be carrying more responsibility than is fair. You need to look at this very carefully because you might have to live with the reality of it for a long time if you marry or if he skips out as soon as you get pregnant. You might reconsider where this relationship is going or get your parents to challenge this young man to prove that he is worthy of your love. He could change.

Another example is not so easy. Perhaps your parents do not want you to date outside of your denomination or religion or culture. No matter how nice this guy is, they may flatly refuse to give you their blessing. Remember that marriage is not only the marriage of two people but the marriage of two families. It is difficult enough to succeed in marriage without the added problem of families that don't support you.

Count the cost. Look what life would be like ten or more years down the road. Will your love carry you through it all if your family is not supportive? All I am saying is to carefully consider your choice for a mate that does not include your parents' blessings.

I personally do not date anyone romantically unless my spiritual mentors or parents **both** approve. I understand that the heart can do silly things when swept away in the currents of passion. I know these people love me more than life itself and want only the very best for me. I trust their judgment. If my spiritual parents don't approve, I would not go out with that person anymore. That's what I would do, but you have to make up your own mind.

My boyfriend looks at pornography a lot.
He wants me to look at it with him.
I don't want to. Am I old fashioned?

No, you are not old fashioned for not looking at pornography. Pornography is one of the fastest ways to destroy relationships and marriages. It seems from your question that your boyfriend is addicted to porn. If he doesn't get help, it will only get worse. There is no bottom to the type of porn that will be needed to turn him on after awhile.

Please look at Chaper 3 which talks quite extensively about the destructive nature of pornography. Also check the Directory where he can get help for his problem. Men who regularly look at pornography tend to look at women as sex objects. A woman wrote to Ann Landers saying that her husband could not make love to her unless he looked at porn first. Is he making love to his wife? No. He is fantasizing about another woman and then uses his wife's body to finish what was started in his head. That kind of sexual union is not a celebration of marriage. That kind of sexual union is not even a celebration of love. It is absolutely selfish.

Hot Lines For The Nineties

How do I tell my boyfriend that I don't want to be sexually active?

The best way to deal with this is straight on and say you are not ready for this kind of relationship. Listed below are gentle, humorous and blunt ways of telling him you are not ready.

He says: "Everybody's doing it"

You say: "Well, if everybody's doing it, you should have no trouble finding someone else!"

or: "I'm not, so that means everybody is not doing it!"

or: "If everybody is jumping off a cliff, it doesn't mean I have to!"

or: "There are certainly enough teenage pregnancies to say that a lot of teens are having sex."

He says: "Let me make a woman out of you!"

You say: "Well, my dog has sex, but that never made a woman out of her!"

or: " I don't have to prove anything. I know what I am".

or: "Woman enough to save all of this passion for the man I marry. Won't he be happy I waited!"

or: "If a woman has to have sex to prove she's a woman, then she doesn't feel very good about herself!"

He says: "I'm a man, I have to have sex!"

She says: "Mice have sex. That doesn't make them men!"

He says: "If you get pregnant, I'll marry you!"

She says: "Marriage is a long way off for me".

or: "I don't want to get pregnant or married
           right now".

or: " Why wait. Let's get married now!"

**My girlfriend is putting pressure on me to go all the way.
I'm not ready yet but what do I say to her to be cool?**

She says: "What's wrong, are you gay?"

You say: "If I were, I wouldn't waste my time dating you!"

or: "I don't want to get that involved right now.
           I've got too much going for me".

or: "Hmmmm, trying to use words to manipulate
           me! It won't work because I decide what I do
           with my life. OK?"

or: "See this aspirin, well you could fit 5 billion
           of my sperm in this aspirin. I'm very fertile
           and I'm not ready to get you or any one else
           pregnant yet!"

or: "If you mean I'm full of mirth, lighthearted,
           sportive, airy, off-hand, showy, brilliant,
           bright coloured, finely dressed…I certainly
           am *but* if you mean living by prostitution or
           the homosexual lifestyle, I'm insulted that you
           could not see the first meaning".

or: "Oh, are you a member of GAY?"
           The *Generation* of *Abstaining Youth?*
           Great, so am I!"

She says: "Don't you desire/love me?"

He says: "Yes, I desire you,
          but my love for you is greater".

or: "Sex is *never* a true test of love".

or: "I love you too much to take the chance to
          jeopardize either one of our futures.
          If you really love me, you'll understand".

How about some good he/she responses?

He/She says: "It's part of growing up".

You say: "Being adult means accepting responsibility
          for my actions. I'm not ready to accept the
          possible consequences yet!"

or: "I can think for myself and that's grown up!"

*He/She says: "If you won't go all the way with me,
          then we'll have to break up".*

You say: "It's easier breaking up now than going all
          the way and then being dumped!"

or: "If having sex is what's needed to hold us
          together, then it's not a very good relationship".

or: "I doubt we would have lasted much longer
          anyway!"

He/She says: "You owe it to me".

You say: "I don't owe you anything".

or: "True love asks for nothing!"

or: "Paying for favors with my body is not my
          idea of a loving relationship!"

or: "A person who pays *that* way sure doesn't think
          much about themselves!"

*He/She says: "If you don't come across,
          there's a lot more fish in the sea!"*
You say: "Well, go fishing!"

He/She says: "You want to enjoy life, don't you?"
You say: "I can have fun without having sex".

or: "Wow, you've lived a sheltered life to think sex
           is the only way of having fun!"

He/She says: "I'm clean/safe, you can trust me".
You say: "You could have the AIDS virus and not know
          it yet".

He/She says: "If we care for each other, it's not wrong!"
You say: "I care enough to say no".

or: "You're the only one saying it's not wrong.
           My parents say it's wrong and so does God!
           If you can change their minds, I'm all for it!"

or: "If you care for me,
           you won't try to destroy my values".

or: "I have to live with myself and
           I believe it's wrong".

He/She says: "I'll stop when you tell me".
You say: "STOP!"

or: "I want to make decisions with my brains
           not my hormones".

or: "It's hard to stop a runaway train.
           It's even harder to stop runaway hormones!"

He/She says: "Come on, have a drink. It'll get you in the mood".
You say: "I'm in the exact *mood* I want to be in,
          thank you".

or: "You know the old saying, 'If you drink, don't drive?' Well there is another one that says 'If you drink, don't kiss!'"

He/She says: "It will bring us closer together".

You say: "Sex alone doesn't bring us closer together. It's everything else we share".

or: "Really? It doesn't seem to work for dogs. They have a different partner every chance they get!"

or: "Sexual intimacy is like Scotch Tape. You can't keep using it on lots of people and expect it will stick as well as it did the first time. I want to bond with one person and know it will hold".

or: "We can be close in other ways".

or: "Having sex doesn't mean you are having a relationship".

or: "Many people share their bodies because it's easier than sharing their heart".

He/She says: "It's natural".

You say: "So are pregnancy, disease and death. They're all part of nature but I can live without them".

or: "So is kissing and hugging. Let's leave it at that!"

or: "We don't have to go all the way to be natural".

He/She says: "Don't you want to be free?"

You say: "I am free already. Free from worry of pregnancy; free from diseases like AIDS; free from abortion or single parenting; free from guilt. Get the picture?"

or: "Couldn't get any freer than I am.
           Why I'm even free from being sexually
           attached to you!
           Isn't that the ultimate freedom?"

**How do you handle not having sex after having been
sexually active for many years?**

It was easy for the first year because I was hoping my
ex-fiancé and I would get back together. But then, wow,
was I hit with racing hormones! I found that the key was
not to look at the problem but to look at the solution.

Sex is energy. Light and sound are energy. I have
learned that with increased libido or sex drive comes
increased energy which I can use wisely or waste on solo
sex (masturbation).

The solution is not to repress this energy but to redirect
it into positive areas. You could:

• Volunteer. Helping people feels good and uses this
  energy positively.

• Become more active in sports. I weight-lift, swim, ride
  a bicycle, ice skate and backpack in the mountains.

• Take up a new activity to divert boredom.

• Develop solid friendships. I find when I'm in the
  company of friends, I don't think about myself as much
  and I have a good time.

• The problem time is usually between 10 p.m. and
  2 a.m., when I'm alone and can't get to sleep. If I've had
  a fun and busy day then there's usually no problem but
  if I've had a lazy day, it's harder to deal with.

For women, certain times of the month seem to be
worse than others, particularly during ovulation and
just before the menstrual cycle starts. Understanding my
cycle helps me to plan activities in order to divert any
possible problems. It is not easy but I look to the future

rewards I will receive in my marriage. If I did not have this hope, I know it would be even harder to cope with.

Men have it worse because it's not just certain times of the month that seem to be more difficult, it's all the time. I compare a woman's libido or sex drive to slow cookers and a man's libido to a microwave. Men especially have to be careful of what they look at because their point of arousal is eyesight whereas the turn on point for women is touch.

I masturbate at least three times a day and sometimes a lot more. Will anything bad happen to me?

Masturbation is typical of the human race. Typical but less than perfect. It's like lying. Everybody has lied but we all know that lying is not right. It's less than perfect. So it is with masturbation. It's less than perfect.

Suppose a person could not fall asleep at night unless they lied some time during the day. Actually, the more they lied, the more they wanted to lie. Would we not say that person was addicted, obsessed and out of control?

So it is with masturbation. If a day can't pass by without this activity, then the person is addicted. Think about it logically. Even in marriage the average couple has sex about two and a half times a week! How will the partner feel knowing that their spouse is never satisfied with the amount of sex they have?

According to many of the sex studies done in North America, men masturbate an average of 3 times a week. This usually stops when they're in a sexual relationship. Women masturbate an average of 2 times a month! That's a big difference. Masturbation is far more addictive for women than for men because they may find it difficult to experience orgasm with their husband during the normal sex act.

Men who get caught up in excessive regular masturbation are hooked on the orgasm more than the journey.

They may experience premature ejaculation with their partner.

Men who masturbate a lot usually use some form of pornography which is also very addictive and seems to create an insatiable appetite for hard core porn.

Root causes of excessive masturbation:

- Early death or divorce in family. Child becomes afraid to love outward and love channels fold inward to self, which seems to cause this inward expression of sex.

- Early exposure to pornography plants seeds of later addictions.

- Sexual abuse will also mature the body ahead of time, physically and mentally. Masturbation seems to become a pattern.

- Late marriages also create real problems for this generation. Not even 50 years ago, people got married in their teens. They seldom had to struggle with wandering hormones. Today the average age of marriage is 25 years. That gives a single person almost 10 years of having to deal with intense sex drives.

Get Help. Check the directory at the back of the book that lists special centres for sex addiction.

Solutions:
1. Don't go to bed until tired.
2. Avoid any X-rated materials.
3. Work on developing solid best friend relationship.
4. Do volunteer work.
5. Become more sports minded or develop other talents.
6. Remember testosterone is also creative energy.
   If you have lots of hormones, you are probably talented in other areas!

Can a man get AIDS from a woman?

Yes, most definitely. Remember AIDS is passed through people sharing needles as well, which is the second major source of AIDS. The AIDS virus is transmitted through body fluids, including blood and semen.

Did you feel pressured the first time you went all the way?

Absolutely. I believe now that what I experienced was really a form of date rape. Because we had been going out for about a month and I really liked this guy, I overlooked what happened. Because I had been sexually abused by an older man in my teens, I felt unworthy of a good man. He told me he wanted to keep going out with me and he would make a good woman out of me. I felt trapped.

According to the latest studies, over 19% of teens felt they were actually pushed or forced into having sex with their partner. I guess we just accept it. We shouldn't. There are laws that protect women now.

Why is it that girls can be sincere to guys but guys can't be to girls?

It's not that girls are sincere and that guys aren't. It's just more difficult for guys. Remember that when it comes to relationships, women are emotional first then they become physical. Men generally are physical first and then *might* become emotionally attached. So women almost always get hurt in sexual relationships because their emotions are already involved. Sex to a man could have no more emotional attachment to it than shaking hands. A man can walk away far more easily after a sexual relationship ends, unless he becomes emotionally attached; then he actually will hurt more than the average woman. Once a man loves mind, body and soul, his love is far superior to any woman's love. It's just harder for a man to get to that level of loving because his physical attraction gets in the way.

Can a girl get pregnant if she doesn't have an orgasm?

It does not matter what kind of mood the woman is in or whether she has an orgasm or not. Pregnancy depends totally upon the presence of an egg which is released according to hormonal cycles. Please read chapter 2 which explains in more detail how a woman's body works. A woman can know when her body is ovulating by learning Natural Family Planning.

What is date rape?

Date rape occurs when one of the partners does not consent to go all the way but is physically forced to. Men, because of their size, can certainly force themselves on us. Usually, part of the problem is that the woman has already started kissing and petting and wants to stop but the man wants more. Because romance is supposed to be kind of magical and mysterious, little discussion goes on beforehand about how far the partners are willing to go. One doesn't normally say before you have kissed, "We will kiss for 5 minutes and then stop, OK?"

Many guys have just assumed that you'll go as far as you want. If you don't give him a swift kick in his jewels, then he doesn't believe that you really want to stop. Some guys have said that women say no with their mouths and yes with their bodies. That's a very dangerous way of thinking. Hopefully friends would have discussed their values long before they ever kissed.

How do I break up with my boyfriend/girlfriend?
I tried before and he/she threatened suicide so
I'm still going out with him/her but I feel trapped!
HELP!

That is a really tough one! First you must realize that this person does not really love you because if he/she did, your partner would be willing to let you go so you could be happy. Your partner is being very selfish and only thinking about his/her own life.

He/she obviously has other problems that started long before you came along. Your partner probably found that he/she could manipulate people by such tactics as threatening suicide.

If you stay with that person, you will never be free. You are being controlled. If you give into the suicide threat, it is almost impossible to break up later.

Get support. Talk to your parents about your problem. Get them to back you up. Then be absolutely rock solid in your decision. No matter what the partner does, do not give in. Try to avoid seeing him/her so he/she can grieve and start adjusting to life without you. You cannot even be friends at this point because that is not what they want.

If you can get away for awhile, all the better. Remember that the person does not love you by threatening suicide. Love has to be unconditional and absolutely free or it is not love. It's as simple as that.

Get outside support during this time to strengthen your own resolve as well as to have other people encourage you. They can even help your ex to adjust to life without you. Explain the situation in the most loving way possible. Even if the person does try something, remember you are not to blame. Each of us makes choices in life and there are consequences to those choices.

The next time, be very careful about declaring eternal love to a person before you really know him/her.

Note: Straight Talk works with a lot of couples who go through the love test. Often the couples agree to separate. Other times one person just walks out on the other and the partner is left with a broken heart. If you suffer a broken heart, we are here to help you. Please read chapter 11 for more information about grieving.

Chapter 13

Warning: Don't Read, It's Religious!

I dedicated this book to a very special teen who impacted on my life to such an extent as to cause a 180 degree change. I also dedicated it to teens across Canada because I think teens are cool. They are super smart and very sensitive and compassionate people. Teens are so full of dreams and high ideals. The world is new and ever changing to them. Nothing is too big to accomplish. I find teens love to be challenged too. If you are a teenager reading this book, I salute you. This book would never have been written but for you teens. I love you.

I'm here today because a teenager that I hired to work the summer of 1981 dared to be different! Not only was she different, she accepted me totally and loved me unconditionally. She was from a Mennonite background but was attending an interdenominational church on the University of Waterloo campus. Karen was going to university and was working during the summer to finance part of her schooling.

At that time I was the manager of a restaurant in Waterloo, called Shantz Country Pork, across the road from Wilfred Laurier University. Depending on the weather I drove to work either in my new car or on my 750 cc motorcycle. I had been living with a young man for approximately five years. He was communistic in his views which was quite natural considering his father was very active in the Communist Party in Yugoslavia and his mother was a practicing Moslem.

We had bought a very large house that was temporarily made into a triplex. We didn't need all the room as there were only the two of us. I coached mixed league baseball, was part of the multi-cultural scene, and an environmental activist. I was only active in the women's movement as far as general equality and was not looking to put women in power for the sake of power. My energies were more concentrated on the global mess of our environment.

I was not ashamed of my lifestyle. I didn't lie about living with my fiancé. It was the way life was for me and many of my friends. It was not the way of life for my fiancé's friends or family but he sure didn't mind!

God was not a part of my life. I was agnostic in my views. I figured if there was a god, one could not really get to know him/her/it so why bother pretending to be religious if it didn't make any sense.

I must confess Christianity held no appeal, as I had seen little in the life of Christians that would challenge me to the truth. They seemed to have as many struggles with life, immorality, drunkenness, etc. as the non-Christian. There was no power, victory or spiritual wholeness which was important to me at the time.

I did go through a spiritual crisis in my early twenties. I felt a real void in my life, even though I had a boyfriend, money, and two businesses of my own; still I felt lost. I read a book called *Zen and Art of Motorcycle Maintenace* which affected me greatly. Probably because this guy rides a motorcycle and travels across United States in search of quality.

Well, I wasn't too interested in quality, but because of my spiritual vacuum, I decided to get on my motorcycle and travel across the Eastern provinces in search of meaning. I lived in a rooming house in Dartmouth, Nova Scotia for about six months. I worked one day a week to pay my bills and the rest of the time I studied different religious books from Zen to Yoga to Transcendental Meditation. Nothing seemed to be the truth. There where bits and pieces here and there and concepts that sounded nice but they didn't ring true.

After six months of this and getting nowhere, I decided to head back to Ontario and get on with my life. I figured if there was a God, he could not condemn me, because I had at least taken time to seek him and God didn't reveal Himself to me. That was His fault, not mine.

On returning to Kitchener-Waterloo, I found work and started dating a friend of mine, who would later become the man I chose to marry; the communist one. Five years later, Karen came to work for me.

One day I was talking to someone about personal problems, and she came over to me in the kitchen and simply said, "I want you to know that God loves you". That took a lot of guts for a person to go to her boss, someone like me, and say that. I was blown away.

I turned on her and said "Are you one of those Born Again Christians?" We always used to laugh at those people. Karen said she was. I then asked her if she believed in the Bible and she answered in the affirmative. I asked her where God was. She answered that He is everywhere.

I figured I had her now. I said to her, "If God is everywhere, then where was He when someone I loved very much was raped? Where was God during the difficult times in our family? Where was God when one of my sisters gave birth to a baby girl who had no stomach? Where is God when all the other horrible tragedies happen around the world. If He is everywhere, then He sees it and *does absolutely nothing*". I was yelling at her, I guess with all the anger that I really had at God, which I couldn't really throw at Him. I decided to give it to this person who seemed to speak on His behalf. I was angry.

Karen was smart, because she kept really quiet. She just stood there. I'm sure she was praying under her breath. She waited until I was finished blowing off steam and gave me an answer that not one person had ever given to me before. It was so simple, yet so powerful in it's wisdom. She had to have been divinely inspired. Karen answered, "God is the same yesterday, today and forever. He is also everywhere. God is in the same place that He was when His only son Jesus Christ was crucified".

I couldn't answer her. She shut my mouth. If she, being a Christian, believed that Jesus was God's only son and God did not interfere in His crucifixion, who was I to complain about my problems? I was just a human being. Well, nothing happened, but I decided to really watch this girl. She seemed different than other young people and she seemed different than most so-called Christians (or should I say church people?).

There is a big difference. Church people just put on spiritual clothes to look spiritual on the outside. Now Karen seemed to be different because she talked about God as her Father. She talked about God in the context of a relationship, not rules and ceremonies and traditions. Her God was not a genie in a bottle to rub a certain way to get your three wishes but a caring Father who seemed to be very involved in our daily lives.

This really intrigued me because Karen was a very intelligent person. Most university students I met threw away their childhood religion along with their toys. But Karen talked the talk and walked the walk. I used to ask some of her co-workers if she was really as straight as she seemed. Some of us called her a Jesus freak or Bible thumper. Yet the more I laughed at her, the more I admired her courage to remain true to her God no matter what the cost. Karen had also said that she was not going to be sexually active until she was married. She felt that sex was a gift not to be unwrapped until the wedding night. I was impressed.

Even though my lifestyle was totally contrary to her beliefs, Karen was always careful to remind me that I could change, that God loved me no matter what, that Jesus died on the cross for my sins and that there was always hope. She said I could start over.

Karen told me after I became a Christian that she and many of her friends at church were praying for my salvation. I guess you could say I was their summer project.

Now Karen really started to get under my skin. Even if she didn't talk about God, just looking at her would cause me to think about God. I couldn't get away from it. The more I tried to resist her God, the angrier I behaved towards her. I was confused because I was normally a pretty good manager. People liked me. I was kind of radical and different but I always had lots of friends. My own behavior towards her upset me.

I remember one day, when Karen just seemed to get under my skin a little too much. Everything she did seemed wrong. I put a lot of pressure on her during the lunch hour to work faster. I guess in a way, I wanted her to swear at me, so I could turn around and say, "Ha, you call yourself a Christian!" But the harder I was on Karen, the nicer she was to me. I couldn't get over it.

After the lunch rush was over and I was finished picking on her, Karen came up to thank me. I was quite surprised. She said "Bev, I want to thank you. [Can you imagine?] I want to thank you for challenging me to excellence because I want to do my work as unto the Lord Jesus Christ!" (Wow, blow me away!)

No matter what I said or did, Karen was always gracious, gentle and very loving. It had to be supernatural!

Karen went back to school in September and I went on with my life. My fiancé had decided that he did not want to turn 30 and not be married, so he had given me until the end of the year for us to get married. By October, I realized, I should call up City Hall and make an appointment to get married. I figured we could get married in the morning and go to work in the afternoon. You know, see if any one would notice.

Anyway, I made an appointment to be married at Cambridge City Hall on October 13, 1981. When I told my fiancé what I had done, I didn't get the reaction I expected. He was not pleased about getting married on the 13th, plus he thought a date closer to Christmas would be better because he wanted to take me on a honeymoon. So I cancelled the 13th and rescheduled our wedding for December 22nd, 1981.

Little did I know that the stage was being set. God had heard my prayers in that attic years earlier and was finally going to pay me a visit.

I went to work on the 13th of October just like I would any other day. No one else knew that we were to have been married on that day. I hadn't told any one. It was no big deal to me. Anyway, Karen called me up that morning, rather distressed. She said that she had been praying a lot for me during the last few days. I hadn't heard from her in awhile and was startled by her comments. She figured that something was going on in my life and that God had burdened her to pray for me. That was very weird, especially since no one knew of my cancelled marriage and she of all people called me out of the blue.

After talking for a few minutes, Karen invited me to get together with her the next day to talk about her school and so on. For some reason, I couldn't say no. There was no great friendship, yet I wanted to see her. She is fifteen years younger than I am!

That evening Karen prayed with some of her friends about the meeting that would take place the next day. They prayed that Karen would have boldness to declare the gospel to me. They prayed that I would have an open mind and an open heart to receive the truth. (Karen and I have compared notes).

That same evening, I drove home to Cambridge and arrived around 8 p.m. My fiancé was unusually tired and had gone to bed early. I guess one of those prayers hit him on the head and he was out. Anyway, here I was alone in the living room. I just knew that Karen was going to talk about God the next day. I grabbed open a Bible and started flipping through the pages.

I guess you could say I prayed my first prayer. I prayed, "God if you are real, I need to know tonight". I prayed to the God of the Bible, the creator of the universe. I had prayed to many other gods in the past but had never prayed to the God of Abraham, Isaac and Jacob.

In my mind, I was thinking to myself that God could not or would not love me personally. As I flipped through the pages of the Bible, I came across a very famous scripture in John 3:16, "For God so loved the world, that He gave His only begotten Son, that whosoever believeth in Him should not perish, but have ever-lasting life".

In my mind again, I said "Well, that is the world, but can You really love *me?*" Again I was flipping the pages of the Bible. I didn't know how to read such a book. Anyway, a scripture in Jerimiah 1:5 seemed to just shout out at me. It reads, "Before I formed thee in the belly, I knew thee; and before thou camest forth out of the womb I sanctified thee…" I was stunned.

All my life I knew how to compete, how to succeed, how to win, but I never really knew how to love or how to receive love. What I needed to know more than anything else was that God could love me, someone who had two abortions and had broken every commandment. Could God still love me? While reading these scriptures, I sensed a presence in the room. The most loving, holy, perfect, pure and wonderful warm presence.

There are no words to describe that encounter. I melted. I could not fight and resist such wondrous love. It was the richest most fulfilling love I have ever encountered in my life. I'm sure I just got a small taste of the awesome love of God. I was truly undone.

I asked God to favor me with just one more scripture. The pages of the Bible stopped at Matthew 10:29-31. "Are not two sparrows sold for a farthing? And one of them shall not fall on the ground without your Father.

But the very hairs of your head are all numbered. Fear ye not therefore, ye are of more value than many sparrows".

The God of the universe had spoken to my heart. In that moment I had an incredible revelation of what Jesus Christ accomplished for us, but especially for me individually. Christ died in my place for all my sins so that I could have a relationship with God. Christ became sin so that I could become the righteousness of Him who knew no sin.

When I accepted Christ as the answer to all questions, I experienced forgiveness for all of my sins. The guilt that I had been carrying and accumulating for 33 years was lifted instantly. I really did feel born again. Very appropriate words. I was free at last.

I cried for hours at the miracle I had experienced. It is the greatest miracle I believe that anyone can encounter. Greater than healing the sick, or blind or the lame or raising the dead. For in a way I was sick, blind, lame and dead. No other religion can take away the guilt, especially the shedding of innocent blood, but praise God for ever more, I can't say enough of what that evening did to me.

The next morning, I told my fiancé that I had encountered Jesus Christ and could not wait to tell Karen the good news. (She was still unaware of this transformation!) I thought my fiancé would be happy or indifferent to my encounter. I was shocked when he challenged me that I had to make a choice between God or marrying him. He would not accept my following this Jesus Christ. It was an ultimatum. I had to make a choice. I chose to follow Jesus. We settled our finances at the lawyer's office. I left with his old car and my clothes.

After work, I picked up Karen who was with her friend, Leslie at the university. They jumped into the car and Karen introduced me to Leslie and asked me how I was doing. I broke down crying, explaining what had taken place the night before and how my fiancé had challenged me to make a choice, and I had chosen to follow Jesus.

I pointed to the clothes in the back seat and told them that I was going to live with my sister for awhile until I could figure out what I was going to do with my life. One day I had everything by the world's standards and the next day I had nothing. Yet I had everything I needed. I asked Karen if she knew what I was supposed to do now. Well she looked at Leslie and back at me and said, "Well I'm not sure because nothing like this has ever happened before".

I went to their apartment and they called their group leader to come over and question me. I didn't know where to go to church so I joined the students in their Sunday morning worship and felt so much at home that I never left. They were radical in their Christianity and that was right on.

I still thank God every day for the courage that young Karen had to overcome her fears and share such love with her black-leathered motorcycle boss.

This is my story. My faith is stronger than ever. My relationship with the creator of the universe, our heavenly Father, through the work of Jesus Christ, grows richer with the passing years. Passion burns within me for others to know such love.

I read the following little story somewhere and wrote it down because I thought it described so clearly how we humans deal with each other and how God deals with us.

The Pit

A man fell into a pit and couldn't get himself out.
A *subjective* person came along and said:
"I feel for you, down there".
An *objective* person came along and said:
"It's logical that someone would fall down there".
A *pharisee* said: "Only bad people fall into a pit".
A *mathematician* calculated how he fell into the pit.
A *news reporter* wanted the exclusive story on this pit.
A *fundamentalist* said: "You deserve your pit".
An *I.R.S. man* asked if he was paying taxes on the pit.
A *self-pitying* person said: "You haven't seen anything
until you've seen *my pit!*"
A *charismatic* said: "Just confess that you're not in a pit".
An *optimist* said: "Things could be worse".
A *pessimist* said: "Things will get worse!"
Jesus, seeing the man, took him by the hand and *lifted
him out* of the pit.

— source unknown

Appendix I

Birth Control

"Nothing will create such a tragic and simply insoluble problem for mankind — as the totally fruitless attempt to separate sexuality from reproduction. Senseless, meaningless and loveless sexuality has a destructive effect".

Freud

As I travelled across Canada and the United States, speaking in both Catholic and public schools, I heard so many conflicting positions about contraceptives that I decided to do extensive research in this area.

I was surprised to discover that Protestant churches originally spoke out against birth control and helped design the laws accordingly. Then, years later, it was this same group who defied Canadian and American laws to promote artificial contraception. Only after the Protestant position to promote birth control became clear did the Catholic Church stand up and defend abstinence as the only position for those who are unmarried.

My research continued to reveal serious physical, emotional and psychological consequences with any artificial means of contraceptive. On the other hand, I have learned that not only is NFP (Natural Family Planning) the most effective way of spacing a family, but it does not contradict any moral or physical laws either.

Another tradition getting attention dates back to the Old Testament book of Leviticus. This tradition is followed by Orthodox Jews and is being taught by Bill Goddard from the Institute of Youth Conflict. The Levitical tradition teaches total sexual abstinence all during the woman's menstrual cycle plus an additional seven days. Once this time was observed, the wife would prepare herself to be joined again with her husband. Desire for each other would certainly maintain intensity. The first days of coming together correspond to a woman's time of fertility. Knowing that returning to each other sexually brings a possibility of a child prepares the couple mentally to accept being pregnant because there is no physical resistance.

Artificial contraceptives do exactly the opposite when it come to attitudes about children. One or both partners choose an artificial means of birth control. The mental image at that moment is that children are not wanted nor would they be welcomed *but* the sexual act is desired. This says 'I love you as long as you don't give me a child'. The man sees the woman as an object to be used for sexual pleasure. Birth control makes the woman available at any time for the man whether she feels so inclined or not. There is no periodic abstinence or self control. Whenever the urge is there, the other partner is supposed to be available.

The Badgley Report in Canada revealed that contraceptive users make up the largest group of women seeking induced abortions (84.8%). When birth control fails, the couple will be shocked and angry. Acceptance of the pregnancy is resisted because it was never wanted. If the couple are unmarried abortion will probably be the most desired form of dealing with the problem. Pregnancy is compared to a disease and the child is never talked about.

Natural Family Planning also observes periodic abstinence similar to the Levitical Laws: however, if the couple is avoiding a pregnancy, the couple would abstain through the woman's menstrual cycle as well as her fertility cycle. The couple does not separate the sex act from life and pleasure. If they do not want a child, the couple postpones any sexual pleasure until a later date. Couples who use NFP are able to achieve the highest effective rate of avoiding a pregnancy as declared by the World Health Organization (98.5%) and also experience a much lower divorce rate when compared to couples using artificial contraceptives.

The following is an historic overview of birth control:

1860s George Drysdale founded the Malthusian League in England. It was named after Thomas Robert Malthus (1766-1834), an English economist and theologian who became famous through his studies on population and economic issues. This first group disbanded.

1878 A new Malthusian League was formed to promote the ideals of birth control. This group expanded into Europe, Brazil, Cuba, Japan and India.

1900 World Congress on Birth Control met in Paris.

1908 The Lambeth Conference of Bishops of the Anglican Church condemned contraception.

1913 Margaret Sanger established the National Birth Control League of America.

1920 The Lambeth Conference of Bishops of the Anglican Church again condemned contraception.

1920s Some American States established illegal birth control clinics.

1930 The first International clinic on contraceptive methods held in Zurich. Almost 200 types of mechanical contraceptive devices were displayed.

1930 The Lambeth Conference of Bishops of the Anglican Church voted to allow the use of contraceptives under certain circumstances.

1930 Pope Pius XI issued *Casti Connubii,* which was a reaction to the Lambeth Conference and stated in no uncertain terms that contraception was wrong.

1939 Birth Control League of America changed its name to Planned Parenthood.

1958 The Lambeth Conference of Anglican Bishops expanded on the issue of contraceptive allowing contraceptives as long as used "according to Christian principles".

1960 Introduction of the birth control pill. One hundred and thirty-two women used the pill 'Enovid' for one year. Today's pill is one thirtieth the strength of that first pill put on the market.

1960 George & Barbara Cadbury opened the Canadian Planned Parenthood in their home in Toronto. They could not get charity status or United Way funding as birth control was still illegal.

1961 The National Council of Churches gave its backing to unnatural forms of birth control which were still *illegal* in Canada and most of the United States.

1965 The US Supreme Court case of Griswold v. Connecticut said that contraception was a matter between a married couple and that anticontraceptive legislation was unconstitutional.

1968 On July 25, Pope Paul VI issued his encyclical letter *Humanae Vitae* concerning the regulation of birth. He strongly condemned any artificial methods but did promote any natural methods and challenged the medical and scientific community to work more diligently in the area of Natural Family Planning.

1969 Canada changed the Criminal Code section 251 to allow abortions when the life or health of the mother was in danger. A subsection legalized birth control.

1972 The US Supreme Court case of Eisenstadt v. Baird extended the right to use birth control to singles.

The Effectiveness of Artificial Contraception

The first thing we need to understand about any form of artificial contraceptives is that *none* are absolutely 100% effective. Any percentages quoted are based on

100 couples using the product for one year. If a couple starts using a product continuously from the age of 16 until marriage, what do you think would be the odds of avoiding pregnancy for the entire time?

Search out studies that reflect the real effective rate of contraceptives according to the age group that you are in. The following chart shows rates for teens under the age of 18.

No matter how effective the contraceptives are on the market they fail to recognize the fact that 28% of teen pregnancies are intended,[1] a view substantiated by Dr. Harriet McAdoo[2] and reporter Leon Dash.[3]

In-Use Contraceptive Failure Rates
For Teen-Age Girls Under 18 Who Are
Trying To Prevent A Pregnancy

Method of Contraceptive	Chance of at Least One Pregnancy		
	1 yr.	5 yr.	10 yr.
Pill	11%	44%	69%
Diaphragm	32%	87%	98%
IUD	11%	43%	67%
Condoms	18%	64%	87%
Spermicides	34%	87%	98%
No Method	63%	99%	99%

The one year rate is the real failure rate for each type of contraceptive listed. The five and 10 year rates are cumulative probability rates using the binomial probability formula.[4]

According to all the research I have studied, it seems that most birth control works better for adults and best for married couples. Apparently the lifestyle of married couples increases the effective rates of contraceptives. That is seldom told to singles even though the singles market spends the most money on birth control.

Ladies, remember that you are born with several hundred thousand eggs in your ovaries, yet only approximately 450 eggs will mature and be released over the course of your childbearing years. It is especially important for women to remember that these eggs can be damaged by drugs, physical trauma, sexually transmitted diseases, etc. Just one summer of careless fun can create a lifetime of torment.

Women are only able to get pregnant about 5 days each cycle, or 65 days each year. All the effective rates are based on 365 days a year, yet there are 300 days when it is impossible for a woman to get pregnant.

Gentlemen need to respect their bodies. When a young man reaches adolescence, he will be producing 50 million sperm a day with no rest on Sundays! That is over 500 sperm every second of his life under normal conditions. They are so small that 85,000 sperm would fit in the end of a pin head! In each sexual encounter a man may pass from 200 million to 500 million sperm in a race to one egg. Sperm have tails and can move at the incredible speed of one inch every eight minutes. Other times these sperm may hang around and party in the reception area for up to three days before swimming upstream. It all depends on the woman and the type of mucus present in her body.

Remember when one decides on being sexually active and using birth control, there is always the chance of pregnancy! The first time I got pregnant we were using a condom and foam. The second time I was on the pill. Toronto has over 13 birth control centres, yet also has the highest abortion rate in the country, with 13,185 abortions and only 8,995 births in 1988.[5]

At our counselling centre, we have counselled women using almost every type of birth control and still pregnancy has occured. Some couples have used two and even three kinds of contraceptives. Teens who were still virgins became pregnant because some sperm entered the vaginal opening and got to the egg. Other ladies who were sterilized still got pregnant.

Condoms

Remember that 28% of teen pregnancies are intended regardless of the type of contraception used.

Real effective rates for those under 18 is 82% for one year, 36% over 5 years and 13% effective over 10 years.

Possible concerns:
• Pregnancy leading to: keeping the baby, adoption or abortion
• AIDS which can lead to death
• Over 30 other sexually transmitted diseases which are painful, can cause infertility or death
• May lose erection
• Allergic reaction to the rubber
• Dulled sensation
• Certain products combined with the condom cause condom to break within a minute after application

Diaphragm

Remember that 28% of teen pregnancies are intended regardless of the type of contraceptive being used.

Real effective rates for teens under 18 is 68% for one year, 13% over a 5 year period or 2% over 10 years.

Possible concerns:
• Pregnancy leading to: parenting, adoption or abortion
• AIDS which can lead to death
• Sexually Transmitted Diseases which can lead to infertility or death
• Pelvic pain
• Increased rates of vaginal infection
• Cramps

- Urinary retention or bladder symptoms
- Profuse vaginal discharge with a foul smell if left
  in too long
- Must be left in up to 6-8 hours after intercourse
- Can be dislodged during intercourse
- Sensitivity to latex diaphragm

Intrauterine Device (IUD)

Remember that 28% of teen pregnancies are intended regardless of the type of contraception used. Most birth control centres do not recommend IUD's to teens since it may reduce the chances of getting pregnant later in life. Real effective rate of IUD for teens under 18 for one year is 89%, over a 5 year period is 57% and over a 10 year period is 33%.

Possible concerns:
- Spontaneous abortion
- Embedding (roots into the wall of the uterus)
- Pregnancy leading to: parenting, adoption, or abortion
- AIDS which can lead to death
- 30 other Sexually Transmitted Diseases which can lead
  to infertility or death
- Unable to have children later on
- Painful menstruation (Severe Dysmenorrhea)
- Heavy Menstrual bleeding
- Pelvic Inflammatory Disease
- Cramps
- Perforation of the uterus
- Intermenstrual bleeding
- Ectopic pregnancy (outside the womb)
- Fallopian Tube infection (Salpingitis)

RU-486

This is not really a form of birth control as it is only taken after a woman becomes pregnant.

RU-486, the abortion pill was named with the initials of its manufacturer, Roussel-Uclaf. It became legal in France in September 1988. The drug Mifepristone in this pill seems to cause abortion by blocking progesterone from acting in the uterus between fertilization and the 6th to 8th week of pregnancy. In pregnancy, the secretion of the hormone progesterone is essential for maintaining the lining of the uterus. Deprived of progesterone, the uterus sheds its lining, including any fertilized egg that is attached to it. As of summer 1992 RU-486 is still not legal in Canada or the USA.

Research is still under way on this product and other similar "morning after" pills. Failure to abort occurs from 5 to 15% of the time. A consent form is usually issued beforehand stating that if the pill does not work then an abortion will be performed. This releases the manufacturer and clinic of possible lawsuits over deformed babies.

Possible concerns:
- Several deaths have been reported
- Causes an abortion
- Possible birth defects
- Severe cramping
- Nausea
- Vomiting
- Prolonged bleeding from 12 - 42 days.
- Diarrhea
- Uterine pain
- Prolonged hemorrhage requiring a blood transfusion

Spermicides
(Vaginal Foams, Creams, Jellies, Suppositories)
Remember that 28% of teen pregnancies are intended regardless of the type of contraception used.

Real effective rates for those under 18 is 66% for one year, 13% over 5 years and 2% over 10 years.

Most public health brochures encourage the use of a barrier method (ie: condom, diaphragm, etc.) along with foam or jelly, yet little mention is made of the high failure rate. Dr. Richard Gordon, a theoretical biologist at the University of Manitoba warns individuals of the high risk of pregnancy over a five year period using the best products under laboratory conditions.

All of the above named products are chemical barriers designed to prevent sperm from entering the uterus. Spermicidal barriers *must* be used for each sex act and should not be inserted more than 30 minutes before intercourse. Most literature does not recommend either bathing or douching for at least 6-8 hours after intercourse to avoid removing the spermicide.

Note: The cervix changes conditions during fertile and infertile periods. During a woman's infertile time spermicidal barriers are not required. When the female is fertile her cervix opens wide to receive as much sperm as possible and the mucus is of a different composition to coat the sperm and protect them from the spermicide. This special mucus feeds and hides the sperm. Sperm have been known to live for up to 72 hours under proper conditions.

Possible concerns:
- Pregnancy leading to: parenting, adoption or abortion
- Sexually Transmitted Diseases
- AIDS which can cause death
- Possible allergic reaction
- Possible birth defects
- Messy
- Can't bath or douche for 6-8 hours after intercourse
- Product must be used before each sex act
- Mercury Poisoning…Phenylmercuric acetate and Phenylmercuric altrate etc.
  (See FDA Federal Register 1979/80)

Sterilization
Tubal Ligation

"Voluntary sterilization means deciding to *forever* give up the capacity to reproduce, regardless of events like the death of your children or divorce and remarriage", notes Dr. Louise Tyrer, vice-president of medical affairs at the Planned Parenthood Federation of America.

In Tubal Ligation, a small incision is made in the abdomen. The fallopian tubes are cut, tied or blocked. The two most commonly used procedures are laparoscopy or mini-laparotomy. The first technique — often called 'belly button' or 'Bandaid' surgery, because the tiny incision is made just inside the navel and covered later by a small dressing. Carbon Dioxide gas is pumped into the abdomen. The physician inserts the laparoscope (a lighted telescope-like instrument) which allows for clear view of the internal organs. The fallopian tubes are either cauterized or pulled into a tiny loop and sealed with a clip or ring fitted around the neck of the loop.

The second procedure involves a small incision into the abdominal cavity where tubes are then divided and ligated. The length of stay in hospital ranges from one to four days depending on the speed of recovery. Both types of procedures prevent the egg from combining with the sperm. Tubal ligation does not result in menopause. The egg is still released monthly along with a menstrual cycle. The egg dissolves in the tube.

Possible concerns:
- Loss of ability to have children
- Pressure on the fallopian tube where egg is dissolving
- 13% will need hysterectomies afterwards
- 36% additional gynecological surgery
- Anesthetic reactions
- 7% ectopic pregnancy (ectopic pregnancy is the leading cause of maternal deaths)

- Slight possibility of pregnancy
- Premenstrual Syndrome
- Endometriosis
- Possible hormonal imbalance
- Painful & heavy periods
- Possible loss of libido (sex drive)
- Sexual dysfunction
- Sexually Transmitted Diseases including AIDS
  if not in monogamous relationship

Male Sterilization
Vasectomy

Vasectomies are usually done in a doctor's office under local anesthetic, normally taking about 20 minutes. The doctor makes a small incision in each of the scrotal sacs to the vasa deferentia (tubes that carry sperm from the testicles to the penis). The tubes are cut and the ends either tied off with suture material, cauterized or sealed with a clip. The man may experience soreness for several days. It takes about a month for the ducts to clear completely of sperm. A semen analysis performed by the doctor will determine when complete sterility has occured. Seminal fluid is still produced but contains no sperm. Failures have been documented between 2 and 10 years after a vasectomy due to what is called a pressure break or "blowout" in the wall of tube.

Possible concerns:
- Loss of ability to produce children
- Potential for STDs if not monogamous
- Potential for AIDS if not monogamous
- 20% of men have feelings of incompetence
- Sperm production still goes on but flows back into body
- Produces anti-bodies against own sperm which can break down immune system
- Allergic reactions to "heparin" given during heart surgery

- Scrota Hematoma
- Infectious and noninfectious Epididymitis
- Possible psychosocial problems
- Postvasectomy pain Syndrome
- Possibility of arthritis
- Possibility of arteriosclerosis
- Infections
- Regrowth of vas deferens (could lead to fertility)
- Premature ejaculation
- Psychological distress
- Sexual dysfunctions

Note: This is a relatively recent procedure, therefore findings are not conclusive. Many studies are still ongoing.

Oral Contraceptives

Remember that 28% of teen pregnancies are intended regardless of the type of contraception used. The pill is a drug so if you are thinking of using it please read this section thoroughly. There are 59 side effects including death, from the pill so it is **very important** to be informed. Also, the **23 drugs that may neutralize the pill** are listed in this section. Please be informed. I have researched hundreds of documents, research papers and government reports.

The real effective rate for teens under the age of 18 is 89% for one year, 56% over a 5 year period and 31% effective over a 10 year period.

There are well over forty different oral contraceptives on the market today. Most of them are what are known as Combined Pills. The other types are known as Mini-Pills and the Biphasic or Triphasic Oral Contraceptives.

Oral Contraceptives contain synthetic hormones which affect hypothalamic, pituitary and ovarian function. Medicine has known for around thirty years about the subtle interrelationship in a negative feedback system among the various hormonal glands under the guidance of the pituitary gland. The pituitary is the relay station between all hormone glands and psyche. This master gland produces more than a dozen other chemicals and hormones, each regulating a vital body process, such as thyroid activity, water metabolism, and body growth. The balance of our body ecology is heavily disturbed through pill-induced synthetic orally active hormones.

According to Barbara Seaman's book, "The Doctor's Case Against the Pill", the pill is dangerous because "it alters every cell and organ in the body. Prolonged use of the Pill can cause a wide range of symptoms. The Pill can cause hair loss, stroke, depression, blindness, skin blotches, skin cancer, bleeding gums, thyroid and pituitary tumors and growth of facial hair".[6]

Oral Contraceptives work in at least 4 ways.

1. Alteration of the physical and chemical properties of the cervical mucus, thereby inhibiting sperm penetration.

2. Endometrial changes hindering implantation (This is an abortifacient action).

3. Inhibition of ovulation.

4. Subtle changes in the hypothalamic-pituitary-ovarian axis with possible altered corpus luteum function. The steroid profiles quite often indicate either an absence of or insufficient luteal activity, or a significant and gradual decrease in several of the indices of luteal function.

Note: The above four points as well as the possible concerns which follow come directly from "The Report on Oral Contraceptives, 1985" by the Committee on Reproductive Physiology to the Health Protection Branch, Health and Welfare Canada, September, 1985.

Possible concerns:
• Thrombophlebitis (blood clot which can lead to death)

- Pulmonary Embolism (can cause sudden death due to blockage of the pulmonary artery or its large branches)
- Mesenteric Thrombosis (clot in the flat, fan-shaped sheet of tissue which carries nerves and blood vessels and supports the intestine, from the "handle" of the fan attached to the back wall of the abdomen)
- Neuro-ocular Lesions (Inflammation of a nerve or it parts in eye area due to toxins, infection, compression, or other causes...temporary or permanent blindness)
- Myocardial Infarction (heart attack)
- Cerebral Thrombosis (clot in cerebrum which is the main part of the brain)
- Cerebral Hemorrhage
- Hypertension
  (abnormally high arterial blood pressure)
- Benign Hepatic Tumors
- Gall Bladder Disease
- Congenital Anomalies (birth defects to future children)

The above are listed as the serious adverse reactions.

The report goes on to list the less serious adverse reactions. These are:
- Nausea
- Vomiting
- Gastrointestinal symptoms
  (such as abdominal cramps and bloating)
- Breakthrough bleeding
- Spotting
- Change in menstrual flow
- Dysmenorrhea
- Amenorrhea during and after treatment
- Temporary infertility after discontinuance of treatment
- Edema (excessive accumulation of watery fluid in body cavities and spaces around cells)
- Chloasma or Melasma
- Breast changes: tenderness, enlargement and secretion

- Change in weight (increase or decrease)
- Endocervical Hyperplasias
  (overgrowth of tissue in cervix)
- Cholestatic Jaundice
- Migraine
- Increase in size of Uterine Leiomyomata
- Rash (allergic)
- Mental depression
- Reduced tolerance to carbohydrates
- Vaginal Candidiasis
- Premenstrual-like syndrome
- Intolerance to contact lenses
- Change in Corneal Curvature (steepening)
- Cataracts
- Optic Neuritis
- Retinal Thrombosis
- Changes in Libido (higher or lower sex drive)
- Chorea
- Changes in appetite
- Cystitis-like syndrome
- Rhinitis
- Headache
- Nervousness
- Dizziness
- Hirsutism (abnormal hairiness of body parts
  not normally hairy)
- Loss of scalp hair
- Erythema Multiforme
- Erythema Nodosum
- Hemorrhagic Eruption
- Vaginitis
- Porphyria
- Impaired Renal Function
- Raymaud's Phenomenon
  (reddening of fingers and toes)
- Auditory Disturbances

- Hemolytic Uremic Syndrome
- Pancreatitis

The President of Ortho Pharmaceutical, Mr. Percy Skuy said in an article in the Globe and Mail, Oct. 13, 1987:

The Pill is not recommended for women who *smoke or are over 35* plus any that have a history of any of the following:"
Poor Circulation
Blood Clots
Stroke
Heart Disease
Artery Disease
Hepatitis
Liver Disease
Breast Cancer
Genital Cancer
Migraine
Diabetes
Gall Bladder Disease
Mononucleosis
Sickle Cell Anemia
Cardiac Disease
Alcoholism
Retardation
Psychiatric Disorders
Depression
Epilepsy
Asthma
Acne
Varicose Veins

If anyone in your family has experienced any of the above problems, it is not advisable to go on the pill.

Complaints about the pill should be forwarded to:
The Birth Control Victims Assoc. Intern.
7 Four Winds Drive, Unit 14
Downsview, Ontario M3J 1K7   (416) 661-6935

Very Important

There are drugs that when taken while a person is on the pill may cause the pill to become ineffective. Please note the following drugs:

Phenobarbital
Carbamazepine
Ethosuximide
Phenytoin
Primidone
Ampicillin
Penicillin
Griseofulvin
Chloramphenicol
Metronidazole
Neomycin
Nitrofurantoin
Sulfonamides
Tetracycline
Rifampicin
Benzodiazepines
Barbiturates
Chloral Hydrate
Glutethimide
Meprobamate
Antacids (All varieties)
Phenylbutazone
Antihistamines
Analgesics
Antimigrane Preparations

Anticonvulsants: reduced efficacy of OCs (oral contraceptives) occurs primarily due to induction of hepatic microsomal enzymes causing reduced circulating levels of contraceptive steroids. Also, increased levels of sex-hormone-binding globulin (SHBG) results in decreased free-circulating hormones.

    Phenobarbital
    Carbazazepine
    Ethosuximide
    Phenytoin
    Primidone

Antibiotics: Altered intestinal flora and "intestinal hurry" (resulting in reduced enterohepatic circulation) have been implicated in reduced OC efficacy.
    Ampicillin
    Penicillin

Stimulation of hepatic metabolism of contraceptive steroids may occur.
    Griseofulvin

Induction of hepatic microsomal enzymes.
Also disturbance of enterohepatic circulation.
    Chloramphenicol
    Metronidazole
    Neomycin
    Nitrofurantoin
    Sulfonamides
    Tetracycline

Increased metabolism of progestogens.
Suspected acceleration of estrogen metabolism.
    Rifampicin

Sedatives and Hypnotics, Tranquilizers: Induction of hepatic microsomal enzymes.
    Benzodiazepines
    Barbiturates
    Chloral Hydrate
    Glutethimide
    Meprobamate

Antacids: Decreased intestinal absorption of progestogens.
    All Varieties

Other Drugs: Reduced OC efficacy has been reported.
Remains to be confirmed.
   Phenylbutazone
   Antihistamines
   Analgesics
   Antimigrane Preparations

Note that oral contraceptive manufacturers recommend using another method of birth control while using above compounds!

Drug Whose Action May Be Modified
by
Oral Contraceptives

Aminocaproic Acid (inhibitor of fibrinolysis): Theoretically a hypercoagulable state may occur because OCs augment clotting factors. *Should not be given with OCs.*

Anticoagulants: Because the estrogen component augments coagulation factors, increased dosages of anticoagulants may be required. Paradoxically, OCs potentiate the action of anticoagulants in some patients.

Antihypertensives:
Guanethidine: Antihypertensive effect is reduced.
Methyldopa: Estrogens cause sodium retention.
Beta Blockers: Increased drug effect due to decreased metabolism.

Betaminetic Drugs:
Isoproterenal: Estrogens cause decreased response to these drugs.
Corticosteroids: Estrogens enhance anti-inflammatory activity. This may retard the metabolism of cortisol. Excessive corticosteroid effects should be watched for.

Cholesterol Lowering Agents:
Clofibrate: The action of these agents maybe antagonized by OCs.

Meperidine: Possible increased analgesia and CNS depression due to decreased metabolism of meperidine. Use combination with caution.

Oral Hypoglycemics, Insulin: OCs may decrease glucose tolerance and increase blood glucose. Increased dosage of hypoglycemic medication maybe required.

Tranquilizers:

Phenothiazines & Reserpine: Estrogens potentiate the hyperprolactinemic effect of these drugs which may cause mammary hypertrophy and galactorrhea. Also potentiation of the ataractic effect of promazine has been reported, possibly due to enzyme induction.

Chlordiazepoxide, Diazepam, Lorazepam & Oxazepam: Increased effects of these drugs may occur due to decreased metabolism.

Alcohol: Increased blood levels of ethanol or acetaldehyde have been reported.

Folic Acid & Vitamin B12: OCs have been reported to impair folate metabolism and reduce serum levels of vitamin B12.

Drugs That May Potentiate The Adverse Effects of Oral Contraceptives

The following drugs all may cause hepatic enzyme inhibition which may potentiate the action of OCs by delaying their metabolism. This may increase the incidence or severity of adverse effects of OCs.

ASA	Methylphenidate
Allopurinol	Mao Inhibitors
Chloramphenicol	Pas
Disulfiram	Phenothiazines
Isoniazid	

Appendix II

Character Identity Determination

Character analysis is based on the principle that every person is made up of three major components. These are body, mind and soul. Character is the sum total of ways we act and react to all things that touch or effect us, in patterns and ways that are very individual, typical and personal. The personal individual and inner force that triggers specific actions or reactions are called "drives".

All reactions register on the human person through their senses — their eyes, ears, smell and touch. These impacts are then transmitted to the brain and experienced as sights, sounds, feelings, as well as ideas, impressions, images, experiences — and finally as emotions, likes and dislikes.

There are two ways the mind functions.

1. Logically, slowly, carefully, analyzing everything, checking out all our decisions and actions for all possible advantages, disadvantages and consequences. This takes time and energy, so consequently this type of mind is deep but narrow.

2. Intuitively, impulsively, quickly grasping oversights and seeing the broad picture. This is a synthesizing type mind. It is broad but superficial.

There are 8 very distinct, very clearly differentiated and easy to understand character types. It takes 50 questions to grasp the insights required of each character. It takes less than 30 minutes to complete and provides between 50-250 pages of information about a person.

This science has been so perfected and is so practical that in France one is not allowed to be a social worker, teacher, counsellor, priest or minister without this training.

For copies of this questionnaire, contact:
Straight Talk
922 Pape Ave., Suite 200
Toronto, Ontario M4K 3V2
(416) 465-9322   (416) 463-9360 (fax)

Appendix III

Studies on Sexual Activity,
Chastity and Divorce

Canada: Youth and AIDS Study, 1988
Health and Welfare Canada

Data for this analysis was obtained from interviews with
over 38,000 Canadian youth (aged 11-21) with respect to
sexual activity, AIDS and STDs.

Detailed information divided teens into groups of
sexual activity. This study is 144 pages in length.

Example: Age 16: Virgins 52%
                   Had sex once/twice 29%
                   Regularly sexually active 19%

Reasons for not having sexual intercourse by gender for
college/university students:
(Detailed table found on page 90 of Study)

Reason	Male	Female
Not Ready	14%	21%
Religion	11%	12%
Fear of Pregnancy	5%	7%
Fear of AIDS	5%	2%
Fear of other STDs	1%	0%
Parents disapproval	1%	2%
Friends disapproval	0%	0%
Virgin until marriage	3%	10%
Not right person	28%	24%
Other	30%	23%

Reasons given by college/university respondents for first
having sexual intercourse by gender.
(Complete table found on page 91 in Study)

Reasons	Male	Female
Expected by Friends	4%	2%
Maintain Relationship	1%	6%
Curiosity	19%	15%
Drugs and alcohol	6%	6%
Passion	12%	7%
Loneliness	1%	1%
Love	27%	52%
Physical Attraction	28%	9%
Other	2%	4%

Number of Sexual Partners:
Tables are found on page 93 of Study. In summary 65% of
sexually active college/university males and 47% of
females indicated that they had sexual intercourse with
three or more partners.

National Opinion Research Center (NORC)
University of Chicago
Data for this 1988 study was drawn from 1,481 adults
across the United States. The findings included:

Sex Partners
The average American adult will have 7.14 sex partners
from age 18 on. Currently married (5.72), never married
(8.67), separated (11.75), and divorced (13.30). The number
of partners was highest in the 40-49 age group.

Abstinence
About 22% of the Adult American population (over 18)
had no sex partners that year. Abstinence was reported
twice as frequently by women (28%) as by men (14%).

Marital Fidelity
About 75% of Americans consider sexual relations with
someone other than one's spouse as always wrong. In any

given year, only about 1.5% of married people have a sex partner other than their spouse. In this survey, men and women did not vary in their levels of fidelity.

[**Note:** Teens are more conservative than adults with 97% of teens expecting to marry and not divorce. 89% of teens consider sexual relations with someone other than one's spouse as always wrong according to the 1991 Bibby Report. Bibby is a sociologist at the University of Lethbridge in Alberta.]

Sexual Orientation
The survey found that 98.5% of sexually active adults have been exclusively heterosexual during the last year. The survey acknowledges that the number is considerably below the 10% adult homosexuals that the Kinsey Report claimed and argues that a 2% homosexual figure is "in line with the best available figures" found in other 1988 studies.

Frequency of Sexual Intercourse
American adults report engaging in sexual intercourse 57 times a year, with the greatest frequency among married couples and separated individuals. Married people under 30 have sex most frequently, 105 times a year.

Urban Institute of Washington, D.C.,
Nationwide survey of 1,880 boys ages 15-19 conducted in 1988.

Teenage Sex
Sixty per cent of teen boys reported experiencing intercourse at least once during the year. The average sexually active teen spent at least six months with no sexual partners. Only about 20% report multiple relationships within the same month. On the average, teen boys said they had intercourse 2.66 times a month, with lowest

average reported by 15-year-olds (1.79 times monthly) and the highest by 19-year-olds (3.45 times a month).

About 11% of American teens said they had their first sexual experience by age 14; 21% by age 15; 58% by age 17; 66% by age 18; and 79% by age 19.

Fifty-seven per cent of the sexually active said they used condoms.

Mel Poretz & Barry Sinrod Survey
Data from this nationwide study conducted in 1991 with 3,144 respondents is published in a book called "Do You do it with the Lights On?"

Frequency of Sexual Intercourse Among Marrieds
Average number of times married couples have sex is 2.74 times per week. The average time spent each week in sexual intimacy is 1 hour, 16 minutes and 34 seconds.

Statistics on Birth Control
The Universal Almanac, 1992
Sixty per cent of all women ages 15-44 use some method of birth control according to U.S. Dept. of Health and Human Resources. (Remember that not all women are sexually active in this category).

The total U.S. female population aged 15-44 is 57,900,000. Of these 35,760,000 are contraceptive users.

Contraceptive Method Used by Marital Status

Method	Single	Married	Divorced
Pill	59.0%	20.4%	25.3%
IUD	1.3%	2.0%	3.6%
Diaphragm	4.9%	6.2%	5.3%
Condom	19.6%	14.3%	5.7%
Other	7.0%	8.4%	5.7%
Sterilization (F)	6.4%	31.4%	50.7%
Sterilization (M)	1.8%	17.3%	3.6%

Birth/Abortion Statistics

Sources are from the Canadian Global Almanac, 1992 and the Universal Almanac, 1992.

Figures are from the census bureaus of Canada and the United States.

Canada, 1986

Total live births to marrieds:	289,386
(Marrieds 15-44 = 4,445,000)	
Total live births to unmarrieds:	79,922
(Unmarried 15-44 = 1,905,000	

Note: Not all unmarrieds are sexually active

Total   369,308

80.5% of all teen births to singles
36.8% of all 20-24 yr. births to singles
14.4% of all 25+ yr. births to singles.

Total abortions to marrieds	18,500
Total abortions to unmarrieds:	61,935

Total   80,435

United States

Total live births to marrieds:	3,266,000
Total live births to unmarrieds:	913,000

Total   4,179,000

National Center for Health Statistics reports that of the nearly 16.2 million births to ever-married women that occurred from 1983 through 1988, about 5.8 million, or 35% were unintended. The most recent statistics show an apparent increase in unwanted births for the first time since the widespread acceptance of the most effective methods of contraception. Between surveys conducted in 1973 and 1982, the proportion of recent births to ever-married women that were unwanted at the time of conception was cut almost in half, from 14.3% to 7.7%. However, the most recent data suggest that the proportion has once again risen to over 10%.

Total abortions to marrieds:		274,257
Total abortions to unmarrieds:		<u>1,097,028</u>
	Total	1,317,285

Divorce

Teens:

Statistics Canada, 1990 stated that teens have highest divorce rate of any category. Four times higher than national average. The length of marriage before divorce is 12.4 yrs.

US Census Bureau claims that 33% of all divorces are couples married less than 5 yrs. and almost 67% of divorces are couples married less than 10 yrs. Divorce rates are highest for teenage wives.

Living Together:

Study No. 1

A Swedish study in 1981 based on a survey of 4,996 women. The study included both those who lived with their future husbands before marriage and those who did not. Couples who lived together before marrying have almost an 80% higher divorce rate than those who didn't. It appears that people who cohabit premaritally are less committed to the institution of marriage and are more inclined to divorce than people who don't live together, according to Neil Bennett, Sociologist at Yale University and one of the study's three authors. Swedes were chosen because they tend to precede American social trends by 10 to 15 years, said co-researcher David Bloom, an economics professor at Columbia University in New York.

Study No. 2

Wisconsin researchers Larry L. Bumpass and James Sweet, drew conclusions from an analysis of the National Survey of Families and Households, which in 1987 and 1988 interviewed 13,017 people about marriage and cohabitation. They found an 80% higher divorce rate among couples who had lived together compared with those who hadn't.

Marry Because of Pregnancy
Jaynanne M. Payne, National Director of the Freemen
Institute of Salt Lake City, Utah states in an article called
"Know the Choices & Consequences" that the divorce rate
for couples who marry because the woman is pregnant
experience a divorce rate of 76%.

Successful Marriages
Average age at marriage:

	Canada	US
Female	28.8	23.9
Male	31.4	26.1

Religious Marriages:
Couples who are married in church and continue to
regularly attend church have a 1 in 50 divorce rate of 2%
and of couples who are married in church and continue
to attend church and also have a prayer life at home,
only 1 in 1,105 gets divorced according to the 1981 U.S.
census figures.

Marriage Preparation:
Charisma Magazine, April 1990 reported that in Modesto,
California an entire church community refused to marry
anyone in their churches unless they have had an inten-
sive marriage preparation course. Number of engaged
couples who break up before the wedding is 50%. Number
of couples who divorce after this preparation is 4.5%.

Ingredients of Successful Marriages:
In June 1985, *Psychology Today* published the results of
a survey. They asked couples married 25 years or more,
"What keeps your marriage going?" Both men and women
gave the same answers in the identical order!

1. **My spouse is my best friend**
2. I like my spouse as a person
3. Marriage is a long term commitment

4. Marriage is sacred
5. We agree on aims and goals
6. My spouse has grown more interesting
7. I want the relationship to succeed
8. An enduring marriage is important to social stability
9. We laugh together
10. I am proud of my spouse's achievements
11. We agree on a philosophy of life
12. We agree about our sex life
13. We agree on how and how often to show affection
14. I confide in my spouse
15. We share outside hobbies and interests

Chastity/Virginity

Studies/articles that support low divorce rate among virgin/secondary virgin marriages:

1. Studies done by Dr. Ray E. Short, professor of sociology at the University of Wisconsin in Platteville.

2. Studies done by Kinsey and others, (Sexual Behavior in the Human Female, pp. 427-28) show that couples who have had premarital sex are more likely to have extramarital affairs. The Kinsey Report shows that women who had sex before marriage were more than twice as likely to cheat on their husbands as women who were virgins at the time of their marriage. Adultery is still the leading cause of divorce.

3. Studies from the American Institute of Family Relations, Los Angeles, including an excellent article by Paul Popenoe called 'Are Virgins out of Date?'

4. Book of Vital World Statistics published by Random House (1990) gives divorce rates for countries around the world. Divorce is mainly a developed world phenomenon; Bermuda and the USA have the highest

rates. Countries that honoured virginity in marriage had the lowest divorce rates, lowest percentage of illegitimate births and lowest abortion rates.

Also note that the value of virginity in marriage is tied very closely to the strength of the religious life of the country. It is almost impossible to separate the two.

Religious life in Canada and the United States is more of tradition than of practicing belief which explains the high divorce rates.

Germany
A poll conducted by the Hamburg Sex Research Institute indicates that young women in Germany are rejecting sexual permissiveness in favor of chastity. The survey, published in *Quick* magazine, found that one in every three German women aged 18 to 25 has not had sexual intercourse.

Sixty-four per cent of those polled considered virginity important, and 96% placed great value on sexual fidelity. *Quick* said young women are increasingly seeking permanent relationships based on love and affection.

United States
1. Pollster George Gallup says the sexual revolution of the last 25 years may be coming to a halt. In 1987, 46% of the people surveyed said premarital sex is wrong while in 1985, the figure was 39%. Gallup says the new findings amount to a "trend reversal".

2. A sex survey of 4,000 asked, "If you had your life to live over again, what one thing would you do differently?" The most popular answer was "I would not have engaged in premarital sex" as reported by Nancy Van Pelt for *Insight* magazine published March 21, 1987.

McDowell's Research Digest
Josh McDowell has developed the Why Wait series of books and videos to equip teens to remain chaste until

marriage. His studies indicate the change in how teens are influenced:

1960	1980
1. Mom/Dad	Friends/peers
2. Teachers	Mom/Dad
3. Peers/friends	TV
4. Religious leaders	Teachers
5. Youth leaders	Popular heroes
6. Popular heroes	Religious leaders
7. Relatives	Newspapers/mag.
8. TV	Advertising
9. Newspapers/mag	Youth leaders
10. Advertising	Relatives

Items Teens Consider To Be A Problem

1. Premarital relationships 99%
2. Drug Abuse 85%
3. Alcoholism 71%
4. Suicide 67%
5. Teen Pregnancy 44%
6. Teen porn & prostitution 15%

Rape/Date Rape

Females Abused by Boyfriends
Study 1.
More than 1,600 girls and young women of high school age in Nova Scotia were surveyed by the Nova Scotia Advisory Council on the Status of Women in 1991. The results were:

Boyfriends sexually abused girls 11%
Boyfriends physically assaulted them 18%
Boyfriends emotionally abused them 32%
Boyfriends forced girls to go all the way 19%

Study 2.
In 1985 a survey of 245 women and 194 men at Washington State University found that 5% of the women and 19% of the men did not believe that forced sexual intercourse on a date is definitely rape or that the man's behavior in such a situation is "definitely unacceptable". Reported in the Regina *Leader Post,* Sept. 23, 1985.

Study 3.
Cornell University found that almost one in five "had intercourse against their will…through coercion, threats, force or violence".

Study 4.
A 1987 survey of 1,700 Rhode Island students in grades 6-9 said it was "acceptable for a man to force a woman to have sexual relations if he has spent money on her". One in four boys and one in six girls agreed to above statement. Among the survey's findings: one-half of the students believed that "a woman who walks alone at night and dresses seductively is asking to be raped; 65% of the boys and 57% of the girls in grades 7 through 9 said it is acceptable for a man to force a woman to have sexual intercourse if they have been dating for more than six months; 87% of the boys and 79% of the girls said rape is acceptable if a couple is married". Reported in the *Globe and Mail,* May 3, 1988.

Directory: Where to Go For Support

Chastity/Secondary Virginity Support Counselling
Straight Talk
(416) 465-9322

Pregnancy Support Counselling
Bethany Christian Services
901 Eastern Avenue, N.E.
Grand Rapids, MI., 49503
Toll free # (800) Bethany

Crisis Pregnancy Centres
Call for centre nearest you
(703) 237-2100 (US & Canada)

Birthright International
Call this number for centre nearest you
(416) 469-1111

Adoption Support Counselling
Straight Talk
(416) 465-9322

Post Abortion Counselling
Abortion Recovery Canada
(604) 640-7171

Last Harvest Ministries
2720 Stemmons Frwy #810 South
Dallas TX, 75207
(214) 630-6565

Straight Talk
(416) 465-9322

Sex/Pornography Addiction Recovery Centres
Sexaholics Anonymous
P.O. Box 300
Simi Valley, CA 93062
(805) 581-3343

Sexaholics Anonymous
Box 90501
Signature Plaza Postal Outlet
283 Markham Road
Scarborough, Ont., M1J 3N7

Birth Control Recovery Centres
Birth Control Victims of America
7 Four Winds Drive, Unit 14
Downsview, Ont., M3J 1K7
(416) 661-6935

Sexual Abuse Recovery Centres
Straight Talk
(416) 465-9322

Meninger Institute
Topeka, Kansas
(913) 273-7500

Drug Addiction Recovery Centres
Cocaine Anonymous
(800) 347-8998

Note: For problems not listed here, please feel free to call Straight Talk and/or call the "Kid's Hot Line"— 1-800-668-6868.

Programs That Promote Abstinence

TEEN-ED
Sandman Plaza, Suite Q
Lethbridge, AB T1J 3L8
(403) 320-8336

TEEN-AID
N. 1330 Calispel
Spokane, WA 99201
(509) 328-2080

Sex Respect or Love Life
Human Life International
Box 7400, Stn. V.
Vanier, Ont., K1J 9M4
(613) 745-9405

Respect, Inc.
P.O. Box 349
Bradley, IL.60915-0349
(815) 932-8399

Postponing Sexual Involvement
Emory/Grady Teen Services Program
Box 26158 Grady Memorial Hospital
80 Butler St. SE
Atlanta, GA 30335

Above program tested by:
    Montreal Council of Women
    1195 Sherbrooke St. W.
    Montreal, Que., H3A 1H9
    (514) 844-7558

It's Cool to Know Your Way in a Relationship
Alberta West Central Health Unit
Box 1718
Edson, AB T0E 0P0

Let's Talk To Teens About Chastity
The Centre for Learning Publications
P.O. Box 910
Villa Maria, PA 16155

Teen Star Program
8514 Bradmoor Drive
Bethesda MD 20817-3810
(301) 897-9323

Note: Texas Council of Family Values used the *Sex Respect* program. After the program, pregnancy was reduced by 2/3; abortion rate was reduced by 1/2 and 70% of students remained chaste through high school.

Note: San Marcos Jr. High in California used the *Teen Aid* program. Before the program there were 178 pregnancies in one year (1 of 5 female students). The first year the program was implemented (1984-85) pregnancies were reduced to 147. The next year of the program (1986-87) saw only 20 pregnancies.

Books to Read

Abraham, Ken. *Don't Bite the Apple 'til You Check for Worms.* Old Tappan, NJ: Fleming H. Revell, 1985.

Burns, Jim. *Handling Your Hormones: The "Straight Scoop" on Love & Sexuality.* Eugene, OR: Harvest House, 1986.

Conway, John F. *The Canadian Family in Crisis.* Toronto, ON: James Lorimer & Company, 1990.

Cook, Barbara. *Love and its Counterfeits.* Lynnwood, WA: Aglow Publications, 1989.

Durfield, Richard and Renee. *Raising Them Chaste.* Minneapolis, MN: Bethany House, 1990.

Fields, Doug, and Temple, Todd. *Creative Dating.* Nashville, TN: Oliver-Nelson, 1986.

Genuis, Stephen, M.D. *Risky Sex.* Edmonton, AB: KEG Publishing, 1991.

Grove, Vicki. *He Gave Her Roses.* Loveland, CO: Teenage Books, 1990.

Haffner, Al. *The High Cost of Free Love.* San Bernadino, CA: Here's Life Publishers, 1989.

Huggett, Joyce. *Dating, Sex & Friendship.* Downers Grove, IL: Inter-Varsity Press, 1985.

Reisman, Judith A. *"Soft Porn" Plays Hardball.* Lafayette, LA: Huntington House, 1991.

Reisman, Judith A. and Eichel, Edward W. *Kinsey, Sex and Fraud.* Lafayette, LA: Huntington House, 1990.

Stafford, Tim. *Love Story.* Wheaton, IL: Tyndale House, 1986.

Trobisch, Walter. *I Loved a Girl.* New York, NY: Harper & Row, 1975.

Trobisch, Walter. *I Married You.* New York, NY: Harper & Row, 1975.

Trobisch, Walter. *Longing for Love.* Wheaton, IL: Crossway Books, 1987.

Van Pelt, Nancy L. *The Compleat Courtship.* Hagerstown, MD: Review & Herald Publishing Assoc., 1989.

Whelchel, Mary. *Common Mistakes Singles Make.* Old Tappan, NJ: Fleming H. Revell, 1989.

White, Joe. *What Kids Wish Parents Knew About Parenting.* Sisters, OR: Questar Publishing, 1990.

Wittscheibe, Charles E. *Teens & Love & Sex.* Washington DC: Review & Herald Publishing Assoc., 1990.

Birth Control Bibliography

Note: This list was developed from the more than 276 documents which I have studied on this subject. Only books and articles published since 1980 have been included on this list.

Aguilar, Nona. *The New No-Pill, No-Risk Birth Control.* New York, NY: Macmillan Inc., 1985.

Anscombe, Elizabeth. *Contraception and Chastity.* London: Catholic Truth Society.

Antonio, Gene. *The AIDS Cover Up?* San Francisco, CA: Ignatius Press, 1986.

Aral, Mosher and Cates. Contraceptive Use, Pelvic Inflammatory Disease, and Fertility Problems Among American Women. *American Journal of Obstetrics & Gynecology.* (1982): 59-64.

Barton S.E. et al. HTLV-III Antibodies in Prostitutes. *The Lancet.* (Dec. 21/28, 1986).

Bergink, E.W., and Kloostenboer, H.J., et al. Effects of Levonorgestrel and Desogestrel in Low-Dose Oral Contraceptives. *Contraception* (1984): 61-69.

Billings, Evelyn, M.D. and Westmore, Ann. *The Billings Method.* New York NY: Ballantine, 1983.

Bolger, Catherine. Sobering Facts on Sterilization. *Messenger.* (April, 1982).

Boston Women's Health Book Collective. *New Our Bodies, Ourselves.* New York, NY: Simon & Schuster, 1985.

Branden, Nathaniel. *The Psychology of Romantic Love.* New York, NY: Bantam 1981.

Britain's Royal College of General Practitioners. Perils of the Pill. *The Lancet.* (Mar. 7, 1980).

Camper, Bill. The Man Who Began the Vasectomy Scare. *McLeans.* (Oct. 6, 1982).

Cimons, Marlene. Breast Cancer in U.S. Reported at Record Levels. *Toronto Star.* (Feb. 2, 1988).

Corneau, Guy. *Absent Fathers, Lost Sons.* Boston, MA: Shambhala, 1991.

Cosgrove, Gillian. Who Tests the Pill Before We're Told it's Safe to Use? *Toronto Star.* (Oct. 25, 1980).

Crenshaw, Theresa L., M.D. *Teenagers, Sex & Condoms.* Culpeper, VA: National AIDS Prevention Institute.

Cruzen, Susan, M. New AIDS Blood Donor Guidelines. *FDA Talk Paper.* (Nov. 21, 1986): T86-82.

Deer, Brian. The Bogus Work of Professor Briggs. London Times. (Sept. 28 and Oct. 5, 1986). *(Briggs was an eminent British scientist who faked major research on leading brands of the contraceptive pill.)*

DeStafano, et al. Long-Term Risk of Menstrual Disturbances after Tubal Sterilization. *American Journal of Obstetrics & Gynecology.* (1985): 152:835.

Diamond, Eugene F., M.D., and Griese, Rev. Msgr. Orville N. *The AIDS Crisis and the Contraceptive Mentality.* Braintree, MA: Pope John Center, 1988.

Dickey, Richard P. *Managing Contraceptive Pill Patients.* Durant, OK: Creative Informatics, 1987.

Dobson, James. *Dr. Dobson Answers Your Questions.* Wheaton, IL: Tyndale, 1988.

Drug Merchandising. *Contraceptive Update.* (1984).

Dunn, H.P., M.D. *Sex & Sensibility.* Australia: Dwyer, 1983.

Ernst, Siegfried, M.D. The Pill: Solution or Time Bomb? *Human Life International Reports.* (Feb. 1987).

Espinosa, J.C., M.D. *Birth Control: Why Are They Lying to Women?* New York, NY: Vantage, 1980.

Fischl, M.A., M.D., et al. Evaluation of Heterosexual Partners, Children, and Household Contacts of Adults With AIDS. *Journal of the American Medical Assoc.* (Feb. 6, 1987).

Flynn, Eileen P. *AIDS: A Catholic Call for Compassion.* Kansas City, MO: Sheed & Ward, 1985.

Frech, Frances. The Pill and the Medical Making of Epidemics. *Population Renewal Office* Kansas City, MO.

Frech, Frances. AIDS Epidemic Started by Pill? *Human Life International Reports.* (Dec. 1987).

Frisch, Melvin, M.D. *Staying Cool Through Menopause.* Los Angeles, CA: Price Stern Sloan, 1989.

Genuis, Stephen, M.D. *Risky Sex.* Edmonton, AB: KEG Publishing, 1991.

Gifford-Jones, M.D. Questions Often Asked About the Pill. *The Nugget.* (Sept. 13, 1985).

Grant, George. *Grand Illusions: the Legacy of Planned Parenthood.* Brentwood, TN: Wolgemuth & Hyatt, 1988.

Greig, James. D. *AIDS: What Every Responsible Canadian Should Know.* Toronto, ON: Toronto Star Publishing, 1987.

Hafer, Dick, with P.A. Brown. *AIDS is Looking for You.* Stafford, VA: A.K.A. Inc., 1987.

Haffner, Al. *The High Cost of Free Love.* San Bernadino, CA: Here's Life Publishers, 1989.

Hancock, Graham and Carim, Enver. *AIDS: The Deadly Epidemic.* London, England; Victor Gollancz Ltd., 1986.

Harris, Louis and Associates. *American Teens Speak: Sex, Myths, TV and Birth Control.* New York, NY: Planned Parenthood, 1986.

Harrison, Lee. Sterilization - The Number One Birth Control Choice. *Women's World Weekly.* (June 17, 1986).

Hayward, Mark D. and Junichi, Yagi. Contraceptive Failure in the United States: Estimates From the 1982 National Survey of Family Growth. *Family Planning Perspectives.* (Sept./Oct. 1986).

Health & Welfare Canada, Committee on Reproductive Physiology. *The Report on Oral Contraceptives, 1985.* Ottawa, ON: Health & Welfare Canada, 1985.

Hess, Rick and Jan. *A Full Quiver.* Brentwood, TN: Wolgemuth & Hyatt, 1989.

Hilgers, Thomas W., M.D. *Reproductive Anatomy and Physiology for the Natural Family Planning Practitioner.* Omaha, NE: Creighton University, 1989.

Joy, Donald. *Bonding: Relationships in the Image of God.* Waco, TX: Word Books, 1985.

Kippley, John F. *Birth Control & Christian Discipleship.* Cincinnati, OH: Couple to Couple League, 1985.

Kolata, Gina. Who Should Stop Using the Pill. *Glamour Magazine.* (May, 1989).

Lavde, P.M., Beral, V., et al. Further Analyses of Mortality in Oral Contraceptive Users. *The Lancet.* (1981): 541-546.

Levy, Steven. The Birth Control Blues. *Rolling Stone.* (Mar. 4, 1982).

Marsiglio, William, and Mott, Frank. The Impact of Sex Education on Sexual Activity, Contraceptive Use and Premarital Pregnancy Among American Teenagers. *Family Planning Perspectives.* (July/Aug. 1986).

McDonnell, Kathleen, and Valverde, Mariana. *The Health Sharing Book.* Toronto, ON: Women's Press. 1985.

McNamee, Lawrence J., M.D. and Brian F., M.D. *AIDS: The Nation's First Politically Protected Disease.* LaHabra, CA: National Medical Legal Publishing House, 1988.

Michaels, Evelyne. Contraception. *Chatelaine.* (Nov. 1988).

Ministry of Health, Ontario. *Your Guide to Birth Control & Family Planning.* Toronto, ON: Ministry of Health, 1987.

Moore, Patrick. Safe Sex Claims & Liability. *Washington Times.* (May 13, 1987).

O'Malley, Becky. Who Says Oral Contraceptives are Safe? *The Nation.* (Feb 14, 1981).

Ortho Pharmaceutical (Canada) Ltd. Considering the Use of Ortho Oral Contraceptives. Don Mills, ON: Ortho Pharmaceutical, 1985.

Planned Parenthood Federation of Canada. *Birth Control That Works.* Ottawa, ON: Planned Parenthood, 1986.

Pollner, Fran. Experts Hedge on Condom Value. *Medical World News.* (Aug. 22, 1988).

Provan, Charles D. *The Bible & Birth Control.* PA: Zimmer Printing, 1989.

Rauhala, Ann. Head of Drug Company Wants Birth Control Pill "Knocked Off Pedestal". *Globe & Mail.* (Oct. 13, 1987).

Reisman, Judith A. and Eichel, Edward W. *Kinsey, Sex and Fraud.* Lafayette, LA: Huntington House, 1990.

Riches, Valerie. *Birth Control for Youth.* Wicken, England: Family & Youth Concern, 1984.

Ruff, Robert H. *Aborting Planned Parenthood.* Toronto, ON: Life Cycle Books Ltd., 1990.

Scotton, Lindsay. Contraceptives. *Toronto Star.* (July 4, 1989).

Seaman, Barbara. *The Doctors Case Against the Pill.* New York, NY: Dolphin Books, 1980.

Slone, Dennis, M.D. Dangers of Pill Last Nine Years. *New England Journal of Medicine.* (Aug. 1981).

Suzuki, David, with Thalenberg, Eileen and Knudtsun, Peter. *David Suzuki Talks About AIDS.* Toronto, ON: General Paperbacks, 1987.

Swedish Study. Link Between the Pill and Appendicitis? *Chatelaine.* (Jan. 1985).

Toughill, Kelly. Common Methods of Contraception. *Toronto Star.* (July 17, 1986).

Wellings, Kaye. AIDS and the Condom. *British Medical Journal.* Nov. 15, 1986: Vol 293.

White, Margaret, M.D. *The Pill: The Gap Between Promise and Performance.* Wicken, England: Responsible Society Research & Education Trust, 1985.

Wright, A. F. Contraception by Female Sterilization. *British Medical Journal.* June 28, 1980.

Zelnick, Melvin, Koenig, Michael A., and Young, Kim J. Sources of Prescription Contraceptives and Subsequent Pregnancy Among Young Women. Family Planning Perspectives. (Jan./Feb. 1984).

Footnotes

Chapter 1

[1] Poretz, Mel and Sinrod, Barry. *Do You Do It With The Lights On?* New York, NY: Fawcett, 1991.

[2] *Bibby Report.* Alberta, Canada. Spring 1991.

[3] Wisconsin researchers, Larry L. Bumpass and James Sweet, drew their conclusions from an analysis of the National Survey of Families and Households, which in 1987 and 1988 interviewed 13,017 people about marriage and cohabitation as reported in the *Baltimore Sun* by Jean Marbella, July 21, 1989.

[4] Payne, Jaynanne M. *Know the Choices & Consequences.* Salt Lake City, UT: Freemen Institute.

Chapter 2

[1] Ryder, N.B. Contraceptive Failure in the United States. *Family Planning Perspectives.* 5: 133-142, 1973.

Chapter 3

[1] Durden-Smith, Jo and Desimone, Diane. *Sex and the Brain.* 1984. Note that "rapist and exhibitionists have higher testosterone levels than is normal" and that "testosterone levels go up before sex".

Chapter 4

[1] Payne, Jaynanne M. *Know the Choices & Consequences.* Salt Lake City, UT: Freemen Institute.

Chapter 9

[1] *Book of Vital World Statistics.* New York, NY: Random House, 1990. 224-227.

Appendix I

[1] Zelnick, Melvin and Kantner, John F. Contraceptive Pattern and Premarital Pregnancy Among Women Aged 15-19 in 1976. *Family Planning Perspectives*. May/June 1978, pg. 140, Table 3.

[2] *Pittsburgh Courier*. July 21, 1984.

[3] Dash, Leon. At Risk, Chronicles of Teen-Age Pregnancy. *Washington Post*. Jan. 26-31, 1986.

[4] Ruff, Robert H. *Aborting Planned Parenthood*. Toronto, ON: Life Cycle Books Ltd., 1990. pg. 72-74.

[5] *Hospital News*. January 1990.

[6] Seaman, Barbara. *The Doctors Case Against the Pill*. New York, NY: Dolphin Books, 1980.

——————————————— • ———————————————

About the Author:

When Bev Hadland speaks about teens and sexuality, she speaks from experience. At 18 she became pregnant and had an abortion. Four years later, while on the birth control pill, she became pregnant again and had a second abortion.

Several years later Bev abandoned a lucrative career in business administration and computer programming to found STRAIGHT TALK, a youth counselling centre. She is well known across North America as a speaker who can communicate openly and easily with teens about sexuality. Bev regularly appears on national television and radio, and has produced a video entitled "Chastity: A Question of Choice". She gives over 250 talks annually to an audience of over 50,000.